First World War
and Army of Occupation
War Diary
France, Belgium and Germany

2 DIVISION
Divisional Troops
Royal Army Medical Corps
4 Field Ambulance
1 May 1915 - 31 May 1915

WO95/1336/5

The Naval & Military Press Ltd
www.nmarchive.com
Published in association with The National Archives

Published by

The Naval & Military Press Ltd

Unit 10 Ridgewood Industrial Park,

Uckfield, East Sussex,

TN22 5QE England

Tel: +44 (0) 1825 749494

www.naval-military-press.com

www.nmarchive.com

This diary has been reprinted in facsimile from the original. Any imperfections are inevitably reproduced and the quality may fall short of modern type and cartographic standards.

Contents

Document type	Place/Title	Date From	Date To
Heading	No 4 7 A May 1915		
War Diary	Bethune	01/05/1915	01/05/1915
Miscellaneous	Ops In May		
Miscellaneous	No 4 Field Ambulance	01/05/1915	01/05/1915
Miscellaneous	Bethune	02/05/1915	02/05/1915
Miscellaneous	No 4 Field Ambulance	02/05/1915	02/05/1915
War Diary	Bethune	03/05/1915	03/05/1915
War Diary	No 4 Field Ambulance	03/05/1915	03/05/1915
War Diary	Bethune	05/05/1915	05/05/1915
Miscellaneous	No 4 Field Ambulance	05/05/1915	05/05/1915
War Diary	Bethune	06/05/1915	06/05/1915
Miscellaneous	No 4 Field Ambulance	06/05/1915	06/05/1915
War Diary	Bethune	07/05/1915	07/05/1915
Miscellaneous	No 4 Field Ambulance	07/05/1915	07/05/1915
War Diary	Bethune	08/05/1915	08/05/1915
Miscellaneous	No. 4 Field Ambulance	08/05/1915	08/05/1915
War Diary	Bethune	09/05/1915	09/05/1915
Miscellaneous	No 4 Fields Ambulance	09/05/1915	09/05/1915
War Diary	Bethune	10/05/1915	10/05/1915
Miscellaneous	No 4 Field Ambulance	10/05/1915	10/05/1915
War Diary	Bethune	11/05/1915	12/05/1915
Miscellaneous	No 4 Field Ambulance	11/05/1915	11/05/1915
Miscellaneous	Bethune	13/05/1915	13/05/1915
Miscellaneous	No 4 Field Ambulance	31/05/1915	31/05/1915
Miscellaneous	No 4 Field Ambulance	13/05/1915	13/05/1915
War Diary	Bethune	14/05/1915	14/05/1915
Miscellaneous	No 4 Field Ambulance	14/05/1915	14/05/1915
War Diary	Bethune	15/05/1915	15/05/1915
Miscellaneous	No 4 Field Ambulance	15/05/1915	15/05/1915
War Diary	Bethune	16/05/1915	16/05/1915
Miscellaneous	No 4 Field Ambulance	16/05/1915	16/05/1915
War Diary	Bethune	17/05/1915	17/05/1915
Miscellaneous	No 4 Field Ambulance	17/05/1915	17/05/1915
Miscellaneous	Roll Of Officers Admitted No 4 Fd. Ambce 24 His Ended 9am 17/5/15	17/05/1915	17/05/1915
War Diary	Bethune	18/05/1915	18/05/1915
Miscellaneous	No. 4 Field Ambce	18/05/1915	18/05/1915
Miscellaneous	Roll Of Officers Admitted No. 4 Fd Ambce 24 His Ended 9am 18/5/15	18/05/1915	18/05/1915
War Diary	Bethune	19/05/1915	19/05/1915
Miscellaneous	No 4 Field Ambulance	19/04/1915	19/04/1915
War Diary	Bethune	20/05/1915	20/05/1915
Miscellaneous	No 4 Field Ambulance	20/05/1915	20/05/1915
War Diary	Bethune	21/05/1915	21/05/1915
Miscellaneous	No 4 Field Ambulance	21/05/1915	21/05/1915
War Diary	Bethune And Lapugnoy	22/05/1915	22/05/1915
War Diary	Lapugnoy	22/05/1915	22/05/1915
Miscellaneous	No 4 Field Ambulance	22/05/1915	22/05/1915
War Diary	Lapugnoy	23/05/1915	23/05/1915
Miscellaneous	No 4 Field Ambulance	23/05/1915	23/05/1915

Miscellaneous	Lapugnoy	25/05/1915	25/05/1915
Miscellaneous	No. 4 Field Ambce	25/05/1915	25/05/1915
Miscellaneous	No. 4 Field Ambulance	26/05/1915	26/05/1915
War Diary	Lapugnoy	27/05/1915	30/05/1915
Miscellaneous	No 4 Field Ambulance	28/05/1915	28/05/1915
Miscellaneous	No 4 Field Ambulance	29/05/1915	29/05/1915
Miscellaneous	No 4 Field Ambulance	30/05/1915	30/05/1915
War Diary	Lapugnoy	31/05/1915	31/05/1915

No 4. F.A.

May 1915

No 4 F.A.

May 1915

Instructions regarding War Diaries and Intelligence Summaries are contained in F. S. Regs., Part II. and the Staff Manual respectively. Title pages will be prepared in manuscript.

WAR DIARY
or
INTELLIGENCE SUMMARY.
(Erase heading not required.)

Army Form C. 2118.

Hour, Date, Place	Summary of Events and Information	Remarks and references to Appendices
1st May, 1915 BETHUNE	Number of Casualties - 38 Lieut. The Hon. Dermot Browne, 1st Colds. Gds., (Colitis) 2nd Lt. H. S. B. Bosanquet, 1st Colds. Gds., (Influenza) Lt. Col. J. E. Lloyd, 1st Kings, (Influenza) Evacuated by No 7 M.A.C. Capt. H. Beddingfield, D.S.O. R.A.M.C., evacuated to No 10 Stationary Hospital, St. Omer, suffering with Suspected Cerebro-Spinal-Meningitis. = (Diagnosis later from St. OMER = Influenza) PHJ	

(73989) W4141—463. 400,000. 9/14. H.&J.Ltd. Forms/C. 2118/10.

49

Ops in May.

for

Acute appendicitis & Peritonitis.

Strangulated Inguinal Hernia

Ligature of Brachial Artery for partial division by G.S.W. (Capt Nixon)

Acute appendicitis & Peritonitis (Lt Townsend)

X. Ligature of Left Subclavian Artery for G.S.W

Acute appendicitis & Peritonitis.

X Shell wd. Abdomen – Peritonitis – Drainage

X G.S.W. Abd " "

Acute Appendicitis Peritonitis

G.S.W. Urethra & Extravasation of urine Perineal ~~Drainage~~ Section – & Drainage

Amput. of Thigh – for shell wd.

G.S.W. Urethra and Scrotum – Suture of urethra

G.S.W. Extraperitoneal Rectum & Bladder Drainage

G.S.W. Bladder – Suprapubic Cystotomy

G.S.W. leg – Gangrene – Paradoxical amp. below knee

For Gas Gangrene arm – Drainage

X F.B. (shell) in brain – Trephined.

Amput. of arm for shell wd.

G.S.W. Popliteal Artery. Ligatured.

No. 4 Field Ambulance

No. of Sick & wounded, by Units, admitted during 24 hours ended 9. a.m. 1/5/15.

Units – 2nd Div.	Officers		Other Ranks		Remarks.
	Sick	Wndd.	Sick	Wndd.	
2nd Grenadier Gds.	.	.	4	1	To Duty.
1st Irish Gds.	.	.	.	4	1st Irish – 1
A. C. C.	.	.	3	.	7th Kings – 2
5th Kings	.	.	.	3	6th " – 1
1st R. Berks	.	.	5	.	R.E. – 1
7th Kings	.	.	2	.	A.S.C – 1
1st Kings	.	.	.	2	2 [illegible] – 1
R.F.A. D.A.C.	.	.	1	.	M.M.G.S – 1
2nd South Staffs	.	.	2	.	
R.A.M.C. attchd.	.	.	1	.	
41st Bde. A.C.	.	.	.	.	
R.F.A. 47th Bty. D.A.C.	.	.	1	.	
R.E. Signal Sect.	.	.	1	.	
Total.	.	.	20	10	
Other Divisions:					To Light Duty:–
1st Coldstream Gds.	2	.	.	.	
19th London Regt.	.	.	.	2	2nd Gren. Gds. – 1
R.E. (170th Coy.)	.	.	1	.	1st Berks – 2
R.E. (23rd Coy.)	.	.	1	.	7th Kings – 1
24th London Regt.	.	.	.	1	R.E. 170th Coy – 1
Total.	2	.	2	3	

Prevailing disease – Nil
No. admitted with foot trouble – 1.

Evacd. by M.A.C.:–
Officers – 3
Other Ranks. – 23
Retd. to Duty:–
Officers Nil
Other Ranks – 8
Retd. to Light Duty:–
Other Ranks – 5

		Sick	Wndd.
Admitted	Officers	2	.
"	Other Ranks	22	13
Evacuated	Officers	.	3
"	Other Ranks	20	16
Remaining	Officers	10	1
"	Other Ranks	47	20

Officers admitted.

2nd Lt. HON. DERMOT BROWNE 1st Coldstream Gds. Colitis
2nd Lt. J. S. BOSANQUET – do – Influenza

A.D.M.S.
2nd Div. 9. am 1/5/15.

P. H. [illegible]
Capt. R. A. M. C.
O.C. No. 4 Field Amb.

No. 4 Field Ambulance.

Return shewing number of Officers & Other Ranks by Units, evacuated SICK out of 2nd Divnl area, during 24 hours ended 9. a.m. 1-5-15.

Units - 2nd Div.	Officers	Other Ranks	Remarks
2nd Grenadier Gds.	.	3	
2nd Coldstream Gds.	.	1	
~~1st. Irish Gds.~~	.	.	
5th Kings	.	1	
A.C. Corps.	.	1	
2nd South Staffs.	.	1	
1st. R. Berks	.	1	
1st Kings	1	.	
Other Divisions:-			
20th Bat. R.F.A.	.	1	
Total	1	9	

R. A. Lloyd Jones.
Capt. R.A.M.C.
O.C. No. 4 Field Amb.

A.D.M.S.
2nd Div. 1/5/15.

Instructions regarding War Diaries and Intelligence Summaries are contained in F. S. Regs., Part II. and the Staff Manual respectively. Title pages will be prepared in manuscript.

WAR DIARY
or
~~INTELLIGENCE SUMMARY.~~

(*Erase heading not required.*)

Army Form C. 2118.

Hour, Date, Place	Summary of Events and Information	Remarks and references to Appendices
2nd May, 1915. BETHUNE.	Capt. A. W. Addinsell, R.A.M.C. arrived for temporary research work with this Unit. Number of Casualties - 28 Lieut. R. C. Featherstonhaugh, 2nd K.R.R. (Shell wd L Arm & L Leg) evacuated to Ambulance train at Chocques. PAG	

No. 4 Field Ambulance

No. of Sick & wounded, by Units, admitted during 24 hours ended 9 am 2/3/18.

Units - 2nd Divsn.	Officers Sick	Officers Wndd	Other Ranks Sick	Other Ranks Wndd
2nd Grenadier Gds.	.	.	.	1
3rd Coldstream Gds	.	.	2	3
2nd -do-	.	.	2	.
1st R. Berks	.	.	4	1
1st Kings.	.	.	2	2
1st Herts.	.	.	.	3
56th Bty R.F.A.	.	.	2	.
R.F.A. D.A.C.	.	.	1	.
5th Kings	.	.	2	.
~~2nd ... Staff~~	.	.	.	.
7th Kings	.	.	4	.
R.A.M.C. 5 Field Amb.	1	.	.	.
1st R.B.R.	.	.	6	.
Total	1	.	25	10
Other Divisions				
9th Kings	1	.	.	.
R.E. (170th Coy)	.	.	1	.
Total.	1	.	1	.

Remarks

To duty:-
- Gren. Gds - 1
- 5th Kings - 3
- R.A.M.C - 1
- 41 Bde. A.C. R.F.A. - 1
- 170th Coy R.E. - 1
- 15th Coy R.E. - 1

Died - 3 (O.R.)
1 Officer

To Light Duty:
- 3rd Colds. - 1
- 1st Irish - 1
- 2nd Fourth Staff - 1
- A.S.C - 1
- 1st Kings - 1
- 11th Coy R.E. - 1
- 1st Cameron Hdrs - 1
- R.A.M.C 4th FA - 1

Prevailing disease - Influenza
No. admitted with Foot troubles - 2.

Evacd by M.A.C.:-
Officers - 4
Other Ranks - 18
Retd to Duty:-
Officers,
Other Ranks
Retd to Light Duty:-
Other Ranks - 8

		Sick	Wndd.
Admitted	Officers	2	.
-"-	Other Ranks	26	10
Evacuated	Officers	4	.
-"-	Other Ranks	27	7
Remaining	Officers	6	2
-"-	Other Ranks	46	20

Admitted Officers

Capt. H. BEDDINGFIELD. D.S.O. R.A.M.C. No. 5 Field Amb. Suspected Cerebro-Spinal Fever.
Lt. Col. J. E. LLOYD. V.D. 9th Kings. Influenza.

P. A. Lloyd Jones
Capt. R.A.M.C.
O.C. No. 4 Field Amb.

A.D.M.S.
2nd Div. 2/3/18.

No. 4 Field Ambulance

Return shewing number of Officers & Other Ranks, by Units, evacuated SICK, out of 2nd Divnl area during 24 hours ended 9. am 2/5/15.

Units – 2nd Div.	Officers	Other Ranks	Remarks
A. S. C.	.	1	
2nd Grenadier Gds	.	1	
2nd Coldstream Gds	.	1	
1st. K. R. R.	.	1	
5th Kings	.	2	
A. Cycle Corps	.	2	
R. F. A (47th Bty)	.	1	
1 R. Berks	.	1	
1st Kings	1	1	
Other Divisions	.	.	
1st Coldstream Gds	2	.	
Total	3	11	

P. A. Lloyd Jones

Capt R. AMC

OC No. 4 Field Amb

A D M S

2nd Div. 2/5/15.

Instructions regarding War Diaries and Intelligence Summaries are contained in F. S. Regs., Part II. and the Staff Manual respectively. Title pages will be prepared in manuscript.

WAR DIARY

or

~~INTELLIGENCE SUMMARY.~~

(Erase heading not required.)

Army Form C. 2118.

Hour, Date, Place	Summary of Events and Information	Remarks and references to Appendices
3rd May, 1915. BETHUNE.	Number of Casualties - 33	
	2nd Lt. F. L. Johnstone, 2nd K.R.R. " " G. T. Lowden, 2nd Inniskilling Fus Lieut. H. Rosam, 9th London. } Evacuated by No 7 M.A.C.	
	Capt. A. H Wood, 5th R. Sussex " G. H. Hay, 1st L. N. Lancs. " A. G. Russell R.G.A } Returned to duty.	
4th May, 1915. BETHUNE.	Number of Casualties - 30.	
	2nd Lt. J A. D. Hewart, 9th H.L.I. Lieut. A. E. P. Mudge. 2nd Innis. Fus 2nd Lt. S Barker, 117th Batt. R.F.A. " " C. J Tomlin. 22nd London } Evacuated by No. 7 M.A.C.	
	PHG [signature]	

(73989) W4141—463. 400,000. 9/14. H.&J.Ltd. Forms/C. 2118/10.

No. 4 Field Ambulance.

No. of sick & wounded, by Units admitted during 24 hours ended 9 am 3/5/15.

Units - 2nd Div.	Officers Sick	Officers Wndd	Other Rks. Sick	Other Rks. Wndd	Remarks
3rd Coldstream Gds.			.	1	To Duty:-
R.A.M.C. 4th F. Al. (~~2nd -do-~~)			1	.	2nd Gren. Gds - 1
2nd South Staffs.			3	1	A.C.C. - 1
2nd Div. A.C. Corps			3	.	5th Kings - 1
A.S.C. No 2 Coy			1	.	1st Fld Coy R.E. - 1
2nd Grenadier Gds.			3	.	
1st Kings.			1	.	
2nd Worcesters.			1	.	
5th Kings			1	1	
1st R. Berks			2	.	
9th H.L.I.	1	.	.	.	
2nd Innis. Fusls	1	.	.	.	
Hd Qrs. 2nd D.A.C.	.	.	1	.	
Total.	2	.	17	3	To Light Duty:
Other Divisions					
2nd K.R.R	1	.	.	.	2nd Cold. Gds - 1
1st Cameron Hdrs.	.	.	2	.	2nd Sth Staffs - 1
9th London Regt.	1	.	.	.	A.C.C. - 1
23rd -do-	1	.	.	.	
24th -do-	.	.	.	1	
Total.	3	.	2	1	

Evacd. by M.A.C.:-
Officers 1 ~~2~~
Other Rks. - 19

Retd to Duty:-
Officers - nil
Other Rks. - 4

Retd to Light Duty:-
Other Rks. - 3

		Sick	Wndd
Admitted	Officers	5	.
-"-	Other Rks	19	4
Evacuated	Officers	-	1
-"-	Other Rks	[illegible]	5
Remaining	Officers	11	1
-"-	Other Rks	53	19

Admitted Officers.

2nd Lt.	F. L. JOHNSTONE	2nd K.R.R.	Contusion L. Knee
-"-	J. P. D. HEWAT.	9th H.L.I.	Ischio Rectal abscess
-"-	G. T. LOWDEN	2nd Innis. Fus.	Sprain ankle ? Potts Fr.
Capt.	A. J. CLARKE	23rd London	Conjunctivitis
Lt.	W. ROSAN	9th -do-	N.Y.D.

P. R. Lloyd Jones
Capt. R.A.M.C.
O.C. No 4 Field Amb.

A.D.M.S.
2nd Div. 3/5/15

No 4 Field Ambulance.

Evacuation Return 9. am.

Officers - Nil

Other Rks. Lying - 2
Sitting 32 J.B.B.

O.C. No 7. M. A.C.
3/5/15

J B B [illegible]
for Capt. R.A.M.C.
OC No 4 Field Amb.

No 4 Field Ambulance

No. of sick & wounded admitted &c. by Units during 24 hours ended 9.0 AM. 4/8/15.

Units. 2nd Div.	Officers Sick	Officers Wndd	Other Rks Sick	Other Rks Wndd	Remarks
1st. Irish Gds.	.	.	4	1	To Duty:-
2nd Grenadier Gds	.	.	7	.	2nd Gren. Gds - 2
2nd South Staffs.	.	.	4	.	Officers
1st K.R.R.	.	.	1	4	5th R. Sussex - 1
5th Kings	.	.	2	1	1st L.N. Lancs - 1
1st -do-	.	.	1	.	4th Seige Bty. R.G.A. - 1
~~Trench Mortar Section attach. 6th Bde.~~			.	.	Other Rks
9th H.L.I.	1	.	.	.	7th Kings - 1
2nd. Innis. Fus	1	.	.	.	R.E. - 1
2nd Worcesters	.	.	1	.	
A.S.C. (No 4 Field Amb)	.	.	1	.	
Total	2	.	21	6	
Other Divisions:-					To Light Duty:-
117th Bty. R.F.A.	.	1	.	.	2nd Gren. Gds - 1
24th Queens.	.	.	.	1	1st Irish Gds - 1
170th Coy R.E.	.	.	1	.	2nd. Sig. Coy. R.E. - 1
A.C.C. 1/2nd London	.	.	1	.	
Total	.	1	2	1	

Prevailing disease:- Influenza

No. admitted suffering from Dropsy: Nil

Evac^d. by No 7 M.A.C.
Officers - 4
Other Ranks - 21

Ret^d. to Duty:
Officers - 3
Other Ranks - 4

Ret^d. to Light Duty:
Other Ranks - 3

		Sick	Wnded
Admitted	Officers	2	1
	Other Rks	23	7
Evac^d.	Officers	6	1
— " —	Other Rks	21	7
Remaining	Officers	7	2
— " —	Other Rks	55	19.

Officers admitted

Capt. A. H. MENZIES	1/9th H.L.I.	Influenza
Lieut. A.E.P. MUDGE	2nd Innis. Fus^rs.	Inf. of Tonsils.
2nd Lt. J. BARKER	117th Bty. R.F.A.	G.S.W. R. Arm.

P. A. Lloyd Jones
Capt. R.A.M.C.
O.C. No 4 Field Amb

A.D.M.S.
2nd Div. 9. Am
4/8/15

No 4 Field Ambulance

Evacuation Return 3 pm

Officers Lying: 1
Sitting: 3 (4 Servants)

Other Ranks Lying: 4
Sitting: 7.

O.C. No 7 Motor Convoy
4-5-15

W M Lockwood Lt Keane
Capt RAMC
O.C. No 4 Field Amb.

Army Form C. 2118.

Instructions regarding War Diaries and Intelligence Summaries are contained in F. S. Regs., Part II. and the Staff Manual respectively. Title pages will be prepared in manuscript.

WAR DIARY
or
~~INTELLIGENCE SUMMARY~~.
(Erase heading not required.)

Hour, Date, Place	Summary of Events and Information	Remarks and references to Appendices
5th. May, 1915. BETHUNE	The DDMS. 1st ~~Army~~ Corps (PHG) visited the Dressing Station for the purpose of seeing some of the cases under treatment by Capt. Addinsell R.A.M.C. Number of Casualties - 42. Lieut H Elliot, 1st Kings evacuated by No 7 M.A.C. Revd Fr Gwynn returned to duty. PHG	

(73989) W4141—463. 400,000. 9/14. H.&J.Ltd. Forms/C. 2118/10.

No 4 Field Ambulance.

No. of sick & wounded, by Units, admitted during 24 hours ended 9.0 am 5/5/15.

Units - 2nd Div.	Officers		Other Ranks		Remarks.
	Sick	Woundd	Sick	Woundd	
2nd Grenadier Gds.	.	.	3	.	To Duty:
2nd Coldstream Gds.	.	.	1	.	1st. R. Berks - 3
1st Irish Gds.	.	.	.	1	56th Bty R.F.A. - 1
1st R. Berks.	.	.	5	.	44th Bde A.C. R.F.A - 1
R.G.A 6th French Bty.	.	.	1	.	2nd. South Staffs - 7
1st Kings	.	.	1	.	7th Kings - 1
1st K.R.R.	.	.	24	.	1st K.R.R. - 1
2nd Inniss. Fusils	.	.	2	.	Coldstream Gds - 1
R.F.A. 56th. Bty.	.	.	1	.	
2nd Worcesters	.	.	1	1	1 Dead.
3rd Coldstream Gds	.	.	1	.	
Total.	.	.	30	2	
Other Divisions					To Light Duty:
7th London Regt.	.	.	1	.	2nd Coldm. Gds - 1
R.E. (170th Coy)	.	.	2	.	3rd -do- - 4
1st Cameron Hdrs } attch 170th Coy R.E. }	.	.	1	.	1st K.R.R. - 1
22nd London Regt.	.	1	.	.	7th Kings - 2
18th -do-	.	.	.	1	1st Berks - 4
6th -do-	.	.	1	.	2nd South Staffs - 1
1st Scotch Gds.	1	.	.	.	R.E. 170th Coy - 1
Total	1	1	5	1	

Prevailing disease . Influenza.
No. admd. suffering from Dysy. - Nil

Evacd. by No. 7 M.A.C.
Officers - 4
Other Ranks - 7
Retd to Duty:-
Officers - Nil
Other Ranks 10
Retd to Light Duty:-
Other Ranks - 14

		Sick	Woundd.
Admitted	Officers	1	1
-"-	Other Rks	25	3
Evacuated	Officers	2	2
-"-	Other Rks	29	2
Remaining	Officers	6	1
-"-	Other Rks	51	19

Officers Admitted

2nd Lieut. C.J. TOMLIN 22nd London G.S.W. L. Hand.
-do- C. BOYD ROCHFORT 1st Scotch Gds. N.Y.D.

P. A. Lloyd Jones

Capt. R.A.M.C.
O.C. No. 4 Field Amb.

A.D.M.S.
2nd Div. 9.am 5/5/15.

No 4 Field Ambulance.

Evacuation Return 9.0.am.

Officers - Nil

Other Ranks. - Lying - 1
Sitting - 4

O.C.
No 7 M.A.C.
9.0am.
5/5/15.

[illegible signature] Lt RAMC
for Capt R.A.M.C.
O.C. No 4 Field Amb.

No 4. Field Ambulance

Evacuation Return.

Officers: – Lying: – 1
Other Ranks Lying: – 8
Sitting: – 6

O.C. No 7 Motor Convoy.
3pm 5-5-15

Harold ? Murphy
Lieut
for Capt RAMC
O.C. No 4 Field Amb

Instructions regarding War Diaries and Intelligence Summaries are contained in F. S. Regs., Part II. and the Staff Manual respectively. Title pages will be prepared in manuscript.

WAR DIARY
or
~~INTELLIGENCE SUMMARY~~.
(Erase heading not required.)

Army Form C. 2118.

Hour, Date, Place	Summary of Events and Information	Remarks and references to Appendices
6th. May, 1915 BETHUNE	The following is a copy of order received from A.D.M.S. 2nd Division:- "O.C. 4 Field Ambulance. M.D. 599 A. 6th. Extract from 2nd Divn. Op. order No 38 4/5/15. G.O.C. LONDON DIVISION assumes command of the CUINCHY and GIVENCHY points at 6 a.m. on 7th. May. The following units will pass under his command at that hour - 4th. Field Ambulance. (Signed) G. Pritchard Taylor, Capt RAMC for ADMS 2nd Divn 6th May, 15 2.55 pm. The following is a copy of Secret orders issued by Colonel R. R. N. Macleod, A.M.S., commanding R.A.M.C. London Divn "Secret Copy No. 5 No. 3. RAMC operation Orders by Colonel R. R. N. Macleod, A.M.S., Commanding RAMC, London Division, 6th May, 1915. Ref. Combined Sheets. Bethune 1/40000. 1. <u>Intention</u> The G.O.C. takes over command of <u>A</u> Section (CUINCHY) and <u>B</u> Section (GIVENCHY) in addition to Sections <u>C</u>. (FESTUBERT) and <u>D.1.</u> (CHOCOLAT MENIER CORNER) at 6 a.m. 7th. May.	

PAG

(73989) W4141—463. 400,000. 9/14. H.&J.Ltd. Forms/C. 2118/10.

Instructions regarding War Diaries and Intelligence Summaries are contained in F. S. Regs., Part II. and the Staff Manual respectively. Title pages will be prepared in manuscript.

WAR DIARY
or
~~INTELLIGENCE SUMMARY~~.

(*Erase heading not required.*)

Army Form C. 2118.

Hour, Date, Place	Summary of Events and Information	Remarks and references to Appendices
6th May 1915. BETHUNE (Continued)	2. "The following troops leave and come under the command at the above hour. (1) To 2nd Division x x x x x x x x x x x x 4th London Field Ambulance. (2) To London Division No. 4 Field Ambulance x x x x x x x x x x x x x x 3. In accordance with above 4th London Field Ambulance will render all returns to A.D.M.S. 2nd Division from the above hour and date when it will come under his orders. 4. No. 4 Field Ambulance will be responsible for evacuation of A & B sections of the line from 4 p.m. 6th May and will maintain the existing Advanced Dressing Stations at 1 HARLEY STREET and PONT FIXE. The usual returns will be rendered to A.D.M.S. London Division from 6 p.m. 7th May. 5. The 5th London Field Ambulance will take over charge of the dressing station at BEUVRY from No. 5 Field Amb at 3 p.m. on 6th. instant. Detailed instructions have been issued to this Ambulance in a special order (No. 2) 6. The 6th. London Field Ambulance will continue to evacuate C and D Sections of the line maintaining its present advanced dressing station at LE TOURET and TUNING FORK	PHE

(73989) W4141—463. 400,000. 9/14. H.&J.Ltd. Forms/C. 2118/10.

Instructions regarding War Diaries and Intelligence Summaries are contained in F. S. Regs., Part II. and the Staff Manual respectively. Title pages will be prepared in manuscript.

WAR DIARY
or
~~INTELLIGENCE SUMMARY.~~
(*Erase heading not required.*)

Army Form C. 2118.

Hour, Date, Place	Summary of Events and Information	Remarks and references to Appendices
6th. May, 1915 BETHUNE. (Continued)	"7. London Division Report Centre at building formerly occupied by 2nd Division Signals. (MARCHÉ AUX POULETS BETHUNE) and ADMS. at No 63 RUE FREDERICK DE GEORGES. (Signed) R. L. R Macleod Col. AMS. London Division Copy No 1 - Office " " 2 4 Lond F.A. " " 3 6 Lond F.A. " " 4 5 Lond F.A. " " 5 No. 4 Fd. Amb. " " 6 ADMS. 2nd Dvn } By cyclist orderly." PHY. The ~~Surgeon General~~ DMS. 1st ARMY visited the Dressing Station today No. of Casualties - 31. Capt. A. G. Clarke 23rd London 2nd Lt. C. C. Boyd-Rochfort, 1st Scots Guards Capt. R. O. Sanders, 1st. Herts } Evacuated by No. 7 M.A.C.	PHY.

(73989) W4141—463. 400,000. 9/14. H.&J.Ltd. Forms/C. 2118/10.

No. 4 Field Ambulance.

No. of sick & wounded, by Unit, admitted during 24 hours ended 9.0pm 6/5/15.

Units - 2nd Div.	Officers		Other Rks		Remarks.
	Sick	Wndd	Sick	Wndd	
2nd Grenadier Gds.	.	.	2	.	To Duty:-
3rd Coldstream Gds.	.	.	3	1	
2nd Innis. Fus.	.	.	1	6	
2nd Worcesters.	.	.	5	12	1st. K.R.R. - 1.
2nd South Staffs.	.	.	3	.	2nd Gren Gds. - 1
R.F.A. 2nd D.A.C.	.	.	1	.	1st Irish Gds - 1
~~[illegible]~~	.	.	.	.	1st Cameron Hrs. - 1
9th H.L.I.	.	.	.	2	Officer
1st R. Berks.	.	.	2	1	Chaplain attd. Irish Gds.
1st Herts.	1	.	.	.	
Total	1	.	17	22	3 deaths
Other Divisions:-					
R.E. 170th Coy.	.	.	1	.	
24th London Regt.	.	.	.	1	To Light Duty:-
					A.C.C. - 2
					A.S.C - 1
Total.	.	.	1	1	5th Kings - 2

Prevailing disease. Influenza
No. admd. suffering from Dropsy.

Evacd. by No. 7 M. AC.:-
Officers - 1
Other Rks - 25
Retd. to Duty:-
Officers - 1
Other Rks. - 4
Retd. to Light Duty:-
Other Rks. - 5

		Sick	Wndd
Admitted	Officers	1	.
"	Other Rks	18	23
Evacuated	Officers	2	.
"	Other Rks	19	15
Remaining	Officers	5	1
"	Other Rks	50	21

Officers Admitted

Capt. R.O. SANDERS 1st Herts. Regt. N.Y.D.

P. A. Lloyd Jones
Capt. R.A.M.C.
OC No. 4 Field Amb.

A.D.M.S.
2nd Div. 9.0pm
6/5/15

No 4. Field Ambulance.

Evacuation Return 3pm

Officers Lying:-1 } 3 Servants
Sitting:-2 }

other Ranks Lying:-6
Sitting:-8

O.C. No 4 Motor Convoy.
3pm 6-5-15

J M Mudworth
Capt RAMC
O.C. No 4 Field Amb

Army Form C. 2118.

Instructions regarding War Diaries and Intelligence Summaries are contained in F. S. Regs., Part II. and the Staff Manual respectively. Title pages will be prepared in manuscript.

WAR DIARY
or
~~INTELLIGENCE SUMMARY.~~

(*Erase heading not required.*)

Hour, Date, Place	Summary of Events and Information	Remarks and references to Appendices
7th May, 1915 BETHUNE	Accompanied by the ADMS London Division, Commanding Officer inspected the Advanced Dressing Stations. The following is a copy of order from ADMS London Divn "Secret. O.C. No. 4 Field Ambulance 5th London Field Ambulance 6th London Field Ambulance In addition to the Routine Reports, Officers Commanding Field Ambulances will send the following by wire or cyclist orderly as early as possible. The number of wounded received since last wire and remaining at the following hours:- 6 am. noon 9 pm. The first report to be sent ~~by~~ at 12 noon 8/5/15. (Signed) C. J. Martin Major 7/5/15 for ADMS London Divn" The following is a copy of a wire received from ADMS 2nd Divn "4 Field Ambulance - MD 607 - 7. Two Ambulance Barges arrived moored South side Canal PONT DU RIVAGE. ADMS 2nd Divn (Signed) M. A. Holt 4.20 pm. Colonel.	RHG

(73989) W4141—463. 400,000. 9/14. H.&J.Ltd. Forms/C. 2118/10.

Instructions regarding War Diaries and Intelligence Summaries are contained in F. S. Regs., Part II. and the Staff Manual respectively. Title pages will be prepared in manuscript.

WAR DIARY
or
INTELLIGENCE SUMMARY
(Erase heading not required.)

Army Form C. 2118.

Hour, Date, Place	Summary of Events and Information	Remarks and references to Appendices

(73989) W4141—463. 400,000. 9/14. H.&J.Ltd. Forms/C. 2118/10.

Instructions regarding War Diaries and Intelligence Summaries are contained in F. S. Regs., Part II. and the Staff Manual respectively. Title pages will be prepared in manuscript.

WAR DIARY
or
~~INTELLIGENCE~~ SUMMARY.
(*Erase heading not required.*)

Army Form C. 2118.

Hour, Date, Place	Summary of Events and Information	Remarks and references to Appendices
7th May, 1915 BETHUNE (Continued)	(b) Head cases requiring immediate operations and abdominal injuries should be retained in Field Ambulances or Casualty Clearing Stations until special arrangements are made for their evacuation. (c) Moribund cases should not be evacuated from any Unit. 9. Additional personnel (a) Additional personnel which may be required at Field Ambulances for loading and unloading ambulance cars and light duties will be obtained, as far as possible from convalescent Companies. (b) Additional personnel to assist stretcher bearers must, as far as possible, also be drawn from convalescent companies. 10. Classification of Injuries for Transport and Disposal of Kits O.C. all Medical Units will pay particular attention to memoranda already issued on these points. No. 7 Motor Ambulance Convoy will clear F. Ambces. of 1st Corps. (Sd.) R. L. R. Macleod Colonel. 7th May 1915. Number of Casualties - 55. Capt. J. C. J. Smith Evacuated by No. 7 M. A. C. Revd. F. D. MORLEY, Chaplain (Wesleyan) joined this unit for duty	PALG.

(73989) W4141—463. 400,000. 9/14. H.&J.Ltd. Forms/C. 2118/10.

No. 4 Field Ambulance.

No. of sick & wounded admitted, by Units, during 24 hours ended 9.0 am 7/5/18.

Units - 2nd Div.	Officers Sick	Officers Wndd	Other Rks. Sick	Other Rks. Wndd	Remarks
2nd Grenadier Gds	.	.	4	1	To Duty:-
1st Irish Gds.	.	.	.	1	2nd South Staffs - 1
5th Kings	.	.	3	.	R.F.A - " 1
1st - do	.	.	2	.	
A.S.C. 2 Coy	.	.	1	.	
R.F.A 41st Bde.	.	.	1	.	
R.F.A. with A.C.	.	.	1	.	
2nd South Staffs	.	.	2	.	
2nd Innis. Fus.	.	.	2	1	2 died from wnds.
2nd Worcesters	.	.	1	.	
R.E. 2nd Signal Coy.	.	.	1	.	
1st R. Berks	.	.	3	.	
R.G.A. 2th H Batz.	1	.	.	.	
Total	1	.	24	3	
Other Divisions:-					To Light Duty:
4th R. Welsh.	1	.	.	1	2nd Colds. Gds - 1
6th London Regt	.	.	.	1	2nd Gren. Gds - 1
23rd - do -	1	.	.	.	1st R.R.R. - 1
7th - do -	.	.	.	1	2nd South Staffs - 1
					1st Berks - 1
Total	2	.	.	2	1st Cameron Hdrs - 1
					ASC 1/2 London A.C.C - 1.

Prevailing Disease - Influenza
No. admitted suffering from Debility - 1.

Evacd. by No. 7 M.A.C:-
Officers - 3
Other Rks. - 16
Retd. to Duty:-
Officers - Nil
Other Rks - 2
Retd. to Light Duty:-
Other Rks - 7

		Sick	Wndd.
Admitted	Officers	3	.
— " —	Other Rks	24	5
Evacuated	Officers	3	.
— " —	Other Rks	23	2
Remaining	Officers	3	1
— " —	Other Rks	51	25

Officers Admitted

~~Capt A.C. CLARKE~~
Capt F.C.J. SMITH — 26th H.Bty R.G.A. — Varice.
— " — R.S.M. GRINDEL — 23rd London Regt. — Influenza.
Lt. F.D ROUFFIGNAC — 4th R. Welsh. — Influenza

R.A. Lloyd Jones,
Capt. R.AMC.
OC No. 4 Field Am

A.D.M.S.
2nd London Div. 7/5/18.

No. 4 Field Ambulance

Evacuation Return 9. am.

Officers - nil.

Other Ranks - Sitting - 8

[signature]

Lieut
for. Capt R. AMC.
OC No. 4 Field Amb.

OC. No. 7 M. A.C.
9. 0. am 1/5/15

No 4. Field Ambulance.

Evacuation Return: 3pm

Officers:- 1

Other Ranks: Lying: 64 *

Sitting: 11

* This includes 2 Cases Suspected Enteric

O.C. No 1 Motor Convoy 3pm 7-5-15

Basil T.H. Murphy Lieut
for Capt R. [illegible]
O.C. No 4 Fd Amb

Instructions regarding War Diaries and Intelligence Summaries are contained in F. S. Regs., Part II. and the Staff Manual respectively. Title pages will be prepared in manuscript.

WAR DIARY

or

~~INTELLIGENCE~~ SUMMARY.

(Erase heading not required.)

Army Form C. 2118.

Hour, Date, Place	Summary of Events and Information	Remarks and references to Appendices
8th May, 1915. BETHUNE	The following is a copy of a secret communication sent to ADMS. London Divn. "Secret. ADMS. London Divn With reference to extracts from Medical arrangements d/- 6/5/15 of DMS. 1st Army it would greatly facilitate the work of my dressing stations if the DMS 1st Army could be asked and agree to publishing an order to say that seriously wounded wounded officers should be brought in the first place to the Main Dressing Station of No. 4 Fd. Ambce. instead of to the Officers' Dressing Station direct, as all operations and important dressings are done at the main dressing Station. (Signed) A N. Lloyd-Jones Capt. RAMC OC. 4 F.A." 8/5/15 Copy of confidential memo from ADMS. London Divn Confidential. Please note that seriously wounded officers should be sent in the first instance to the Main Dressing Station of No 4 F.A. instead of the Officers Dressing Station direct, as all operations and important dressings are done at the main dressing station and issue the necessary instructions to all Medical Officers under your command. (Signed) C J Martin Major for Colonel 8/5/15.	PHG

(73989) W4141—463. 400,000. 9/14. H.&J.Ltd. Forms/C. 2118/10.

Instructions regarding War Diaries and Intelligence Summaries are contained in F. S. Regs., Part II. and the Staff Manual respectively. Title pages will be prepared in manuscript.

WAR DIARY
or
~~INTELLIGENCE SUMMARY~~.
(Erase heading not required.)

Army Form C. 2118.

Hour, Date, Place	Summary of Events and Information	Remarks and references to Appendices
8th. May, 1915. BETHUNE. (Continued)	Permission was asked of A.D.M.S. 2nd Divn 4/, in view of the fact that all seriously wounded officers of 1st. Corps are to be sent to Officers' Dressing Station, it would be possible to temporarily replace Lieut H.H.P. MORTON, RAMC as we are working one officer short of establishment.	
	Lieut H.H.P. MORTON, RAMC. rejoined for duty from temporary duty with 2nd Heavy Brigade, R.G.A.	
	The following is a copy of a secret order issued by A.D.M.S. London Divn	
	"Secret No 4 Field Ambulance 6th London Field Ambulance DM. 45 - 8. The reports called for yesterday from Field Ambulances of admissions wounded and remaining wounded at 6am. noon and 9p.m. will not be required today AAA They will be rendered from tomorrow, beginning noon AAA (Signed) C.J. Martin Major for A.D.M.S. Lon. Divn"	PHG
	Number of Casualties - 40.	
	Lieut V.D.R. Coulam, A.S.C. returned to duty	

Instructions regarding War Diaries and Intelligence Summaries are contained in F.S. Regs., Part II. and the Staff Manual respectively. Title pages will be prepared in manuscript.

WAR DIARY

or

~~INTELLIGENCE~~ SUMMARY.

(Erase heading not required.)

Army Form C. 2118.

Hour, Date, Place	Summary of Events and Information	Remarks and references to Appendices
8th May, 1915 BETHUNE (Continued)	The following confidential communication from DMS. 1st Army, forwarded through ADMS London Divn "DMS. 865 55. ADMS 2nd London Divn With regard to paras. 4 and 5(a) of Medical Arrangements, 1st Army, issued under my 6/5/15, please note that officers suffering from wounds of the thorax and injuries suitable for conveyance by barge, may also be placed direct on barges. With reference to paragraph 7, the messages at 6am. noon, and 9pm. will commence only from the date upon which definite operations commence. H.Q. 1st Army (Signed) W. G. Macpherson 7/5/15. Surgeon General DMS. 1st Army 2 OC. No 4 Fd. Ambce. Forwarded for your information (Signed) C. J. Martin 8/5/15. Major for Colonel ADMS Lon Divn"	[initials]

(73989) W4141—463. 400,000. 9/14. H.&J.Ltd. Forms/C. 2118/10.

Instructions regarding War Diaries and Intelligence Summaries are contained in F. S. Regs., Part II. and the Staff Manual respectively. Title pages will be prepared in manuscript.

WAR DIARY
or
~~INTELLIGENCE~~ SUMMARY.

(Erase heading not required.)

Army Form C. 2118.

Hour, Date, Place	Summary of Events and Information	Remarks and references to Appendices
8th May, 1915 BETHUNE (Continued)	The following is a copy of secret correspondence from ADMS. London Divn. "To O.C. No. 4 Field Ambulance S 3. 5th London F Amb. 6th London F Amb Enclosed from DDMS. 1st Corps. Should it be found necessary to form this convoy it will be made up as follows No. 4 Fd. Amb. 3 Large Cars. 5th London Fd. Amb. 1 Officer 4 Large Cars 1 Small Car. 6th London Fd. Ambce. 1 Large Car 1 Small Car. (Signed) C. J. Martin, Major for ADMS. Lon. Dv."	
8/5/15	"Copy. DDMS. 1st Corps 82 S 3. ADMS. London Divn. Should entraining of wounded take place at BETHUNE, you will please detail 1 medical officer as entraining medical officer, and 10 cars from your medical units. The arrangements must be made now as notice may be short and the trains must not be delayed over. The duties of entraining Medical Officer will include exclusion of cases likely to die on the journey, and the return of empty stretchers for full ones to the Casualty Clearing Station or Field Ambulance. (Signed) P. G. Easton, Major RAMC for DDMS. 1st Corps 1st Corps. 7th May, 1915.	PHG

(73989) W4141—463. 400,000. 9/14. H.&J.Ltd. Forms/C. 2118/10.

Instructions regarding War Diaries and Intelligence Summaries are contained in F. S. Regs., Part II. and the Staff Manual respectively. Title pages will be prepared in manuscript.

WAR DIARY
or
~~INTELLIGENCE SUMMARY.~~
(Erase heading not required.)

Army Form C. 2118.

Hour, Date, Place	Summary of Events and Information	Remarks and references to Appendices
8th May, 1915. BETHUNE (Continued)	The following is a copy of a confidential memo received from A.D.M.S. London Divn "To O.C. No 4 Field Ambulance. 5th London F. Amb. 6th London F. Amb. The following wire has been received from 1st. Corps. " Cases of Gas poisoning will be shewn under headings of wounded or killed in action but notes should be made intimating nature of injuries so shewn as wounds. (Signed) C J Martin Major for A.D.M.S. Lon. Divn 8/5/15.	PRLG

(73989) W4141—463. 400,000. 9/14. H.&J.Ltd. Forms/C. 2118/10.

No. 4 Field Ambulance.

No. of sick & wounded, by Units, admitted during 24 hours ended 9. a.m. 8/5/15.

Units - 2nd Div.	Officers Sick	Officers Wounded	Other Rks Sick	Other Rks Wounded
2nd Coldstream Gds.	.	.	1	5
[1s]t Irish Gds.	.	.	3	2
[2n]d Grenadier Gds.	.	.	1	.
[1s]t Kings	.	.	5	.
R.E. 2nd Signal Coy.	.	.	2	.
A.S.C. M.T.	.	.	1	.
1st Herts.	.	.	1	.
1st R. Berks.	.	.	3	.
2nd South Staffs.	.	.	7	.
1st Kings "	.	.	7	.
1st K. R. R.	.	.	2	.
2nd H.L.I.	.	.	4	.
R.A.M.C. attached 2nd Colds. Gds	.	.	1	1
26th H.B.ty. R.G.A.	.	.	1	.
R.F.A. 44th Bde. A.C.	.	.	1	.
-"- 22nd Bty.	.	.	1	.
Total	.	.	41	8
Other Divisions:-				
3rd Coldstream Gds	.	.	1	.
2nd Welsh	.	.	1	.
R.E. 1st Field Coy (Mounted Staff)	.	.	1	.
R.E. 170th Coy.	1	.	1	.
22nd London Regt.	.	.	.	1
Total.	1	.	4	1

Remarks

To Duty:-
A.C.C. - 1
R.F.A. - 1
3rd Colds. Gds - 1

To Light Duty:-
2nd Gren. Gds - 14
2nd Worcesters - 1
R.G.A. 6th T. Bty - 1
1st K.R.R. - 2
1st Berks - 3

Other Divns.
3rd Colds Gds - 1
R.E. 170 Coy - 1
2nd R. I. Fus. - 1

1 Death.

Prevailing Disease:- Bronchitis Catarrhal
No. admitted suffering from Dropsy:- 1.

Evacd. by No. 7 M.A.C.:-
Officers - 1
Other Rks - 18
Retd. to Duty:-
Officers - Nil
Other Rks. - 5
Retd. to Light Duty:-
Other Rks. - 14.

		Sick	Wounded
Admitted	Officers	1	.
-"-	Other Rks.	45	9
Evacuated.	Officers	1	.
-"-	Other Rk.	32	5
Remaining	Officers	5	1
-"-	Other Rks.	64	28

Officers admitted

Lt. J.H. Leaming   R.E. 170th Coy.   Constipation.

P. A. Lloyd Jones
Capt. R. A.M.C.
O.C. No. 4 Field Amb.

A.D.M.S.
London Div. 9 am 8/5/15.

No. 4 Field Ambulance

Evacuations Return. 9.0 am.

Officers - Nil

Other Ranks. - Lying - 2

Sitting - 4

[illegible signature]

[illegible signature]

for Capt. R.A.M.C.

O.C. No. 4 Field Amb.

O.C. No. 7 M.A.C.

9 am. 8/5/15.

Instructions regarding War Diaries and Intelligence Summaries are contained in F. S. Regs., Part II. and the Staff Manual respectively. Title pages will be prepared in manuscript.

WAR DIARY
or
~~INTELLIGENCE~~ SUMMARY.

(*Erase heading not required.*)

Army Form C. 2118.

Hour, Date, Place	Summary of Events and Information	Remarks and references to Appendices
9th May, 1915, BETHUNE. (Continued)	The following are extracts from Orders issued by the Commanding officer:- " 2. No wounded officers will be admitted into the French Ward. They may be dressed at the main dressing station but must be moved immediately afterwards. 3. Convalescents 1. of London Division will be sent to London Field Ambulances. 2. of 2nd Division to Convalescent Company at RUE DU COLLEGE. 4. Evacuation. In addition to the instructions posted in the Hall, the following will be carried out. 1. Wounds of the lungs, head cases not requiring immediate operation and severe fractures will be evacuated straight to the Barges at PONT DE RIVAGE. These cases may be put into cars going to officers Dressing Station: report will be made to the office at once when such a case is sent. 2. Head cases requiring immediate operation and abdominal injuries will be reported and brought to the notice of the Commanding officer 3 Moribund cases will not be evacuated	PAL

Instructions regarding War Diaries and Intelligence Summaries are contained in F. S. Regs., Part II. and the Staff Manual respectively. Title pages will be prepared in manuscript.

WAR DIARY
or
~~INTELLIGENCE SUMMARY.~~
(Erase heading not required.)

Army Form C. 2118.

Hour, Date, Place	Summary of Events and Information	Remarks and references to Appendices
9th. May, 1915 BETHUNE	At about 9 am the first wounded were admitted as a result of the attack made by the 1st. Division. Up till 9 o'clock at night a continuous + steady stream of wounded was brought to the Dressing Station. Up till 9 pm. the majority of cases admitted were officers. At about 9 pm. there was a sudden influx of Other Ranks and until about 2·30 am on the following day the admissions did not abate. The total number of casualties from 9 am 9/5/15 to 9 am. 10/5/15 were - Officers - 117. Other Ranks - 146. The number of cases evacuated during the day were:- By No 7 Motor Ambulance Convoy - Officers - 59 Other Ranks 77. Evacuated to Ambulance Barges - Officers 11 Other Ranks 15. Lieut. A MacMillan, 58th. Rifles died from wounds received in action. During the day the Main Dressing Station was visited by DMS 1st Army, DDMS. 1st Corps, ADMS. 2nd Divn and ADMS. London Division. H.R.H. The Prince of Wales accompanied by his Equerry visited the officers' Dressing Station.	[signature]

(73989) W4141—463. 400,000. 9/14. H.&J.Ltd. Forms/C. 2118/10.

Instructions regarding War Diaries and Intelligence Summaries are contained in F. S. Regs., Part II. and the Staff Manual respectively. Title pages will be prepared in manuscript.

WAR DIARY

or

~~INTELLIGENCE SUMMARY.~~

(Erase heading not required.)

Army Form C. 2118.

Hour, Date, Place	Summary of Events and Information	Remarks and references to Appendices
9th. May, 1915. BETHUNE. (Continued)	The following instructions regulating the admissions and evacuations taking place at the Officers Dressing Station were issued by the Commanding Officer:- "Instructions for Officers' Dressing Station 1. Sick Officers or Slightly wounded Officers awaiting evacuation may be taken direct into the Officers' Dressing Station. 2. Only Slightly wounded Officers will receive their first dressings at the Officers Dressing Station. All serious cases will be dressed for the first time at the Main Dressing Station. 3. Sick Officers will be evacuated as soon as possible 4. The lower ward will be used as far as possible for seriously wounded Officers and sick officers awaiting evacuation. 5. Cases unfit to be moved and slightly wounded cases will be placed in the Upper Ward. (Signed) P. A. Lloyd Jones. Capt. RAMC. OC. No 4 Fd. Ambce." 9/5/15	PHG

(73989) W4141—463. 400,000. 9/14. H.&J.Ltd. Forms/C. 2118/10.

No. 4 Field Ambulance

No. of sick & wounded, by Units, admitted during 24 hours ended 9.0 a.m. 9/5/15

Units – 2nd Div.	Officers Sick	Officers Wnded	Other Rks Sick	Other Rks Wnded	Remarks
2nd Grenadier Gds.			3		To Duty:
1st Irish Gds.			1		
2nd Coldstream Gds			2		1st Kings – 1
3rd do			2	1	
5th Kings			1		
7th do			1		
13th do			3		Officer.
1st R. Berks	1		3		[illegible]
2nd Inniskilling Fus.				1	
1st K.R.R.					
1st [illegible] R.B.			1	1	
2nd H.L.I.	1				
2nd Worcesters					
London Irish	1				
Total	3 (4)		3 (4)	3	

To Light Duty:
2nd Grenr. Gds. – 1
2nd Innis. Fus. – 3
2nd Worcesters – 4
2nd South Staffs – 1

Other Divisions	Officers Sick	Officers Wnded	Other Rks Sick	Other Rks Wnded
1st Cameron Hdrs.				1
7th London Regt.				1
2nd Royal Sussex		2		
R.F.A. Lahore D.A.C.	1		1	
31st [illegible] R.E.				
Total	1	2	1	2

Prevailing Disease – Influenza.
No. admitted suffering from [illegible] – Nil

Evacuated to No. 7 M.A.C.
Officers – Nil
Other Ranks – [illegible]

Retd. to Duty
Officers – 1
Other Ranks – 1

Retd. to Light Duty
Other Ranks – 9

		Sick	Wndd
Admitted	Officers	5	2
– " –	Other Rks	27	5
Evacuated	Officers		
– " –	Other Rks	[illegible]	10
Remaining	Officers	4	2
– " –	Other Ranks	1	3

Admitted Officers

2nd Lt. B. CROSSLEY	2nd H.L.I.	[illegible]
– " – E.J.D. TOWNSEND	R.F.A. Lahore D.A.C.	[illegible]
– " – E.P. BENNETT	2nd Worcesters	[illegible]
Lt. G. SEARLES	1st R. Berks	[illegible]
Capt. E.F. VILLIERS. D.S.O.	2nd R. Sussex	[illegible]
Lt. C. de St. CROIX	2nd R. Sussex	[illegible]
Lt. H.T. HUTCHINSON	London Irish	[illegible]

A.D.M.S.
9/5/15.

Capt. R. [illegible]

Instructions regarding War Diaries and Intelligence Summaries are contained in F. S. Regs., Part II. and the Staff Manual respectively. Title pages will be prepared in manuscript.

WAR DIARY
or
~~INTELLIGENCE SUMMARY~~.
(Erase heading not required.)

Army Form C. 2118.

Hour, Date, Place	Summary of Events and Information	Remarks and references to Appendices
10th May 1915. BETHUNE,	Number of Casualties - 34 Evacuated by No 7 M.A.C. - Officers 37 Other Ranks 35. Lieut F. Holmes, 4th R. Inniskilling Fusrs. } Died from wounds Capt. J. Eric Evans, 4th R.W. Fusrs. } received in action. Lieut G. M. Garrod, 1st L.N. Lancs. 2nd Lt D. Pretty, 4th Suffolks, died from injuries sustained to spine and head. The following confidential memo was received from A.D.M.S. 2nd Divn "O.C. 4, 5, 6 Field Ambces. M. 136 - 10. No further evacuations of sick and wounded will take place until 7 M.A.C. is informed that accommodation in Clearing Stations is available. (Signed) M. P. Holt, Colonel, A.D.M.S. 2nd Divn H. Q. 2nd Divn 2 p.m.	PHG

(73989) W4141—463. 400,000. 9/14. H.&J.Ltd. Forms/C. 2118/10.

No. 4 Field Ambulance

No. of sick wounded, by Units, admitted during 24 hours ended 9 a.m. 10/5/15

Units – 2nd Div.	Officers Sick	Officers Wndd	Other Rks Sick	Other Rks Wndd
2nd H.L.I.				1
R.F.A. 7th Mountain Bty.				1
1st King's		1		
1st K.R.R.		1		
2nd Inniskilling Fus.	1			
Total	1	2		2
Other Divisions				
1st N'hants		7		9
3rd -do-				
2nd K.R.R.		4		3
1st Camerons		3		10
9th Gurkhas				1
1st Scots Gds		3		6
2nd R. Sussex		6		13
1st L.N. Lancs		6		9
5th Sussex		6		2
7th London				1
6th -do-				1
A.S.C. London Div.			2	
O.T.C. -do-			1	
9th Kings		2		3
24th London		2		3
2nd Gurkhas				1
2nd Black Watch attd I.E.F.				1
London Scottish				6
1st South Wales Bdrs		2		10
4th R. Welsh Fus.		2	1	1
1st Gloucesters		3		20
1st Coldstream Gds.			1	
2nd R. Munster Fus.		6	1	11
R.F.A.				1
R.E. 1st Field Coy		1		2
2nd Welsh		4		7
3rd South Wales Bdrs				4
1st Black Watch		4		7
1st Seaforth Hdrs		7		1
2nd Black Watch		2		1
4th Seaforths		5		
6th ~~[illegible]~~ Jats.		1		
40th Pathans		1		
Carr fwd.	·	79	6	140

Remarks

To Duty.
- Irish Gds. 1
- 1st Kings – 2
- 2nd South Staffs – 2
- R.Amb. attch 2 Coldm. Gds – 1
- 1st R. Berk – 2
- A.S.C. – 1
- R.F.A. 44 A.C. – 1
- H.L.I. 2
- 12

To Light Duty.
- 2nd Gren. Gds – 3
- 2nd Coldm. Gds – 2
- 2nd Lancasters – 4
- 1st Berks – 2
- [illegible] R.E. – 1
- 9th Kings – 2
- H.L.I. 170 Coy – 1
- 2 South Staffs – 2

No. 4 Field Amb.

No. of Sick & Wounded admitted during 24 hours ended 9. am 10/6/15 (Contd.)

Units. 2nd Div	Officers		Other Rks	
	Sick	Wndd.	Sick	Wndd.
Brot. fwd.		79	6	140
Dublin Frs attd. M'chester Inf.		1		
6th Worcesters attd. Lancs		1		
107th Pioneers		1		
2nd Lincolns		1		
1st Gloucesters attch. Seato Bde		1		
Indian Reserve of Officers		1		
Royal Irish Fusils		1		
3rd Loyal North Lancs		1		
2nd Reserve attch. Gharwal.		1		
9th Bhopals		3		
8th Gurkhas		1		
R.F.A. 51st Bty		1		
London Cyclists	1	.		
4th R. Munster Frs.	1			
2nd Leicesters		2		
4th Suffolks		1		
R.F.A. 20th Bat.		1		
do. 44th Bat.		1		
4th Black Watch		3		
3rd Queens		1		
41st Dogras		2		
2/3 Gurkhas		1		
Total	2	105	6	140

Prevailing disease nil
No admitted suffering from Dysp. nil

Evacd. by No. 7 M.A.C.
Officers - 59
Other Rks - 77
Retd. to light duty
Other Rks - 17
Retd. to Duty
Officers - nil
Other Rks. 12
Evacd. to Barges.
Officers 11
Other Rks. 15

		Sick	Wndd.
Admitted	Officers	2	105
"	Other Rks	6	140
Evacuated	Officers	11	57
"	Other Rks	53	68
Remaining	Officers		49
"	Other Rks	6	95

Roll of Officers admitted to follows.

P. A. [illegible]
Capt. [illegible]
OC No 4 Field Amb.

Nominal Roll of officers admitted
No. 4 Fd. Ambulance 24 hrs ended 9am.
10/5/15.

Rank	Name	Regt.	Wound or Disease
Capt	[illegible]	2 R Sussex	G.S.W. R Leg
2nd Lt.	[illegible] B.		
"	Townsend E. J. D.	R [illegible]	Appendicitis
"	Bennett E. P.	2nd Worcesters	
Lieut	[illegible]	1st R. Berks.	
Capt	St. Croix [illegible]	2nd R Sussex	G.S.W. R Leg
Lieut	Hutchinson H.T.	[illegible] Irish	
2nd Lt.	Clark J.	1st Northants	G.S.W. Back.
Major	Langham P.H.	5th R Sussex	Shell wd Back
Lieut	Napper F. W.	— do —	G.S.W. Eye.
2nd Lt.	H. R. M. Dodd.	— do —	G.S.W. Hand.
Capt.	Sir F V L Robinson	1st Northants	Bay.t Wnd Testicles
Lieut	R S Champion	3rd [illegible] att. 1st Northants	Shell Wnd Back & Hand
"	A P Gordon-Cumming (CUMMING)	1st. Camerons	G.S.W. Arm.
"	A. W. Fulton	9th. [illegible]	" Chest
Capt.	T.P. Aldworth	3rd [illegible] 2nd Welsh	" Arm & R. Thigh
2nd Lt.	P.H. Cummings	1st Seaforths	Shell Wd L. Arm.
Lieut.	C.M. Cameron	4th "	" L. Arm.
2nd Lt.	J. Frederick	1st "	" Back.
Lieut	P. B. Hubbert	6th Jats.	G.S.W. L Shldr.
2nd Lt.	H. H. Forbes	1st Northants	Shell Wnd Eye.
Lieut	W. Fisher	1st [illegible] N. Lancs	" Head
2nd Lt.	E. Johnson	40th Pathans	" L. Arm
Capt	W. D. Daly	Dublin Fusiliers att. Manchester Fus.	" Arm
Lieut	G.S. Nalty	2nd K. R. R.	G.S.W. Leg

Rank	Name	Regt.	Wounded or Disease
Capt.	Hon. A. F. M. Harris	2nd K.R.R.	Chest Wd?
Lieut.	F. H. Crook	— do —	G.S.W. Head & Leg
do	W. H. Roy	[illegible]	[illegible]
Lieut.	J. R. C. A. Hebert?	7th Sussex	Gunshot Wd Back.
do	J. L. Perry	— do —	[illegible]
Capt.	J. E. G. Carlyle?	[illegible]	Back.
Lieut.	F. K. [illegible]	[illegible]	R. [illegible]
2nd Lt.	A. A. Mathews?	1st Scots Gds.	[illegible]
do	A. G. A. Vickers?	2nd R. Sussex	Gunshot Wd Arm
2nd Lt.	R. H. Richards?	[illegible]	Arm & Body
Capt.	[illegible]	[illegible]	Shoulder
do	H. [illegible]	2nd R. Sussex	Arm & Body
do	S. L. [illegible]	[illegible]	G.S.W. Head & Hand?
2nd Lt.	A. Siggery?	9th Kings	L. Arm
do	[illegible] G.B.	1st Glamorg.?	R. Arm
do	[illegible]	1st [illegible]	[illegible] R. Arm
do	W. Dell?	[illegible]	G.S.W. R. Arm
do	J. C. Harman?	1st [illegible]	R. Wrist
do	J. R. [illegible]	24th London	R. Arm?
do	[illegible]worth	[illegible]	R. Shoulder?
do	A. Saunders	[illegible]	Head
do	J. Ball	1st Seaforths?	Head
do	C. J. Balfour	1st Scots Gds.	R. Arm
Lieut.	R. L. [illegible]	2nd K.R.R.	Gunshot Wd Head
Major	T. W. Thomas	9th [illegible]	G.S.W. Head
Capt.	G. E. B. [illegible]	[illegible]	[illegible] Wd Arm
do	Willoughby [illegible]	5th [illegible] R.F.A.	Back.
do	J. E. Harrison?	1st Scots Gds.	Leg.

A.

Rank	Name	Unit	Wound &c.
Capt	T. Stanley	1st Kings	Influenza
[illegible]	S. J. [illegible]	[illegible]	[illegible]
[illegible]	P. C. Hart[illegible]	[illegible] Seaforths	[illegible]
Lieut	[illegible]	[illegible]	[illegible]
2nd Lt	[illegible]	[illegible]	[illegible]
[illegible]	[illegible]		G.S.W. Back
[illegible]	S. M. [illegible]	[illegible]	[illegible] R. Leg
[illegible]	C. H. [illegible]	[illegible]	[illegible]
Capt	M. K. Daniell	[illegible]	[illegible]
Major	H. R. Sargeant	9th Rhodes	Shell Concussion
[illegible]	R. H. H. [illegible]	10th	[illegible]
Lieut	G. E. Wakefield	[illegible] Yorks	Shell wound R. [illegible]
[illegible]	C. M. Cameron	4th Seaforths	G.S.W. Lung
2nd Lt	A. H. H. Hartnell	2nd Sussex	G.S.W. L. Leg
"	G. M. Stephens	4th Suffolk	" R. Arm
"	G. C. Fairbank	1st Glosters	" Neck
"	J. H. Jeavons	1st Glosters	G.S.W. R. Arm
"	J. M. Pender	1st Seaforths	G.S.W. R. Leg
"	N. Evans	[illegible]	[illegible]
"	[illegible] A. Hodges	1st Glosters	G.S.W. Chest
[illegible]	R. A. [illegible]	10th L.N. Lancs	[illegible]
2nd Lt	K. A. Mosher	1st S.W.B.	G.S.W. R. [illegible]
Major	F. M. B. Robertson	[illegible]	G.S.W. [illegible]
2nd Lt	J. Holmes	[illegible]	Shell wnd L arm & groin
"	H. Moore	[illegible]	[illegible]
Major	A. Graham	2nd [illegible]	[illegible]
Lieut	G. M. Garrard	1st L.N. Lancs	G.S.W. [illegible]
"	G. [illegible] de L. Landon	46th Bde R.F.A.	[illegible]

Rank	Name	Regt.	Wound
Lieut	N. R.J. Turner	2 S. W. Borderers.	G.S.W. Head
"	J. E. M. Richards	1st. Bl. Watch	" Abdomen
"	D. Maxwell	R.F.A. 94th Batt	Shell wnd Arm & Leg
2nd Lt.	G. W. Cox.	4th Bl. Watch	" " R. Shdr.
" "	G. G. Moore	2nd " "	" " Arm & Leg
Capt.	E. L. Boase	4th. Bl. Watch	" " L. Arm.
Lieut	P. W. Keating	Connaught Rangers att. 2. R. M. F.	" " L. Arm
"	Hoare C. T.	3rd. Queens	" " Butts & Sacrum
Capt.	A. W. S. Brock	2nd Leicesters	" " L. Arm
Lt. Col.	C. A. R. Hutchinson	41st. Dogras.	G.S.W. Buttock
Capt.	J. Eric Evans	4th. R. W. Fus.rs	Shell wnd L. Leg.
2nd Lt.	C. M. Green	2nd Sussex	Shell wnd Side & Arm
Capt.	C. L. Patton-Bethune	1st. Camerons	Shell wnd Thigh
"	J. E. Fitzpatrick	2nd R. M. Fus.	" " L. Arm
2nd Lt.	T. F. Murdoch	1st. Bl. Watch	G.S.W. R. Shdr. L. Leg.
" "	L. Margrave	2nd Welsh	Wound Concussion
" "	J. A. Nye	1st. Northants	G.S.W. R. Thigh & Shdr.
Capt.	M. W. Hawkes	2nd R. M. Fus.	" Shdr & Arm.
2nd Lt.	F. H. Bowles	1st. Gloucs.	" R. Hand
" "	J. B. T. Haldane	1st. Bl. Watch	Shell W. R. Arm L. Side
Major	J. W. Milne	41st Dogras	" " R. Shdr.
2nd Lt	J. C. Soloman	24th London	Wound concussion
Capt.	M J M Campbell	Connaught Rangers att. 2nd Welsh	G.S.W. Rt finger
"	F. C. Finch	1st Gloucesters	L. Leg
2nd Lt.	G. C. P. Talbot	2nd Sussex	" L. Waist
2nd Lt.	H. St J. Attwater	1st Northants	" Back
Capt	A. G. Stone	3rd Gurkhas	Shell Wnd Head
"	C. C. Myle	1st Northants	G.S.W. R Shoulder

Rank	Name	Reg.	Wound
2nd Lt	G C Morris	1st L.N. Lancs	Wound concussion
" "	S R P Roberts	2 Sussex	Shell Wnd hip + posterior
Capt.	W.D. Hill	1st L.N. Lancs	Shell Wnd back + buttock
Lieut	A. H. Sutherland	2nd Black Watch	GSW L arm
2nd Lt.	R R Mc McDonald	4 Seaforths	GSW. Legs
2nd Lt	G. R. M. Reid	4 Argyle + S'land Hdrs att 2 Black Watch	GSW. Scalp
" "	V. A. Heskett-Smith	1st Camerons	
Col.	C. A Wilding	2nd Innis Fus.	Injury to Knee

Instructions regarding War Diaries and Intelligence Summaries are contained in F. S. Regs., Part II. and the Staff Manual respectively. Title pages will be prepared in manuscript.

WAR DIARY
or
~~INTELLIGENCE SUMMARY.~~
(Erase heading not required.)

Army Form C. 2118.

Hour, Date, Place	Summary of Events and Information	Remarks and references to Appendices
11th May, 1915. BETHUNE	Number of casualties - 56. Evacuated by No. 7 M.A.C. - Officers 11 Other Ranks 44. Capt. J. E. G. Carlisle, 107th Pioneers died from wounds received in action 9/5/15.	
12th May, 1915. BETHUNE.	Number of Casualties - 57. Evacuated by No. 7 M.A.C. - Officers - 10. Other Rks - 32. 2nd Lieut N. E. FORBES, R.F.A. } Died from wounds received 2nd Lieut R. M. CHADWICK, R.G.A. } in action. The following secret order was received from the A.D.M.S. 2nd Divn. "Secret. To 4 F.A., 5 F.A., 6 F.A., 4th Lond. F.A. G.S. 2nd Divn for information. D.D.M.S. 1st Corps for information. D.M.S. Army for information. M. 138. 12 1. No. 4 F.A. passes today under orders of 2nd Divn 2. 4th Lond F.A. " " " " 47th (Lond) Divn 3. No. 5 Field Ambce. will handover ECOLE JULES FERRY to a F.A. of 1st Divn, together with patients unfit to be moved AAA After relief will move to LOCON at 5 pm today and take up billets to be indicated and open one tent Sub Divn. at School there. 4. No 4 F.A. will hand over Advanced Dressing Stations at PONT FIXE and No 1 HARLEY STREET to a bearer Sub. Divn of 1st. Divn about 9 a.m. tomorrow AAA After relief the bearer Sub Divn 4 F.A. will rejoin Unit headquarters. H.Q. 2 Divn. (Signed) M. P. Holt 11.10 A.M. Col. A.D.M.S.	[initials]

(73989) W4141—463. 400,000. 9/14. H.&J.Ltd. Forms/C. 2118/10.

Instructions regarding War Diaries and Intelligence Summaries are contained in F. S. Regs., Part II. and the Staff Manual respectively. Title pages will be prepared in manuscript.

WAR DIARY

or

~~INTELLIGENCE SUMMARY.~~

(Erase heading not required.)

Army Form C. 2118.

Hour, Date, Place	Summary of Events and Information	Remarks and references to Appendices
12th May, 1915. BETHUNE (Continued).	The following order was received from ADMS 2nd Divn "4 F Amb., 4th Gds. Bde. G.S for information DADMS for information II Div M 141 12. OC. 4 F. Amb will detail one bearer Sub. Divn to a company 4th Gds. Bde. tomorrow AAA. Liaison Officer to to report to H.Q 4th Gds. Bde. for instructions forthwith. (Signed) M. P. Holt Colonel ADMS." ADMS. Adv. 2 Div 7.15 pm The following is a copy of secret orders issued to O.C. Bearer Sub. Division, No 4 F.A. You will hand over the Advanced Dressing Station at PONT FIXE and No1 HARLEY STREET to a bearer Sub. Division of a Field Ambulance detailed from the 1st. Divn at about 9am. tomorrow 13th. inst. After being relieved you will rejoin Head Quarters 4 F.A. forthwith. Orders for this move will not be issued until Reveille on the 13th. inst. S.S. Todd RAMC is being sent in temporary relief of Sgt. Money RAMC 12/5/15. (Signed) A. A. Lloyd Jones Capt. RAMC OC. 4 FA. 3 pair of horses will arrive at No1 HARLEY St. at 9 am. Please bring in wheeled Stretchers (Initialled) AALJ	PKLJ

(73989) W4141—463. 400,000. 9/14. H.&J.Ltd. Forms/C. 2118/10.

Army Form C. 2118.

WAR DIARY
or
~~INTELLIGENCE~~ ~~SUMMARY~~.
(Erase heading not required.)

Instructions regarding War Diaries and Intelligence Summaries are contained in F. S. Regs., Part II. and the Staff Manual respectively. Title pages will be prepared in manuscript.

Hour, Date, Place	Summary of Events and Information	Remarks and references to Appendices
12th May, 1915. BETHUNE. (Continued)	The following secret order issued to OC. Bearer Sub-division No.4 Fd. Ambce. W. 144 12. On being relieved by Capt. G. E. Dyas RAMC, you will return to H.Q. 4 F.A. for duty AAA Lieut M. M. McCullagh, RAMC to report at once tonight to H.Q. 4th Guards Bde as liaison officer AAA Please send in both the motor ambulances in your charge. Sgt Money RAMC. is returning tonight please send back to H.Q. S.S. Todd RAMC. One scotch cart and one riding horse for Lieut McCullagh will leave here at 5 am. tomorrow and 3 pairs horses at 8 Am. Please hand over instructions concerning move to Capt. Dyas AAA OC. 4 F.A. (Signed) P.H. Lloyd Jones Capt. RAMC. OC. 4 FA.	PHLJ.

(73989) W4141—463. 400,000. 9/14. H.&J.Ltd. Forms/C. 2118/10.

No. 4 Field Ambulance.

No. of Sick and wounded, by Units, admitted during 24 hours ended 9 a.m. 11/5/15.

Unit Lond. Divn	Officers Sick	Officers Wndd	Other Rks. Sick	Other Rks. Wnd.	Remarks
24th London	–	–	–	2	To Duty:-
1st. Herts.	–	–	–	1	5 Kings – 1
2nd Gren. Gds.	–	–	2	–	1 Berks – 1
3rd Colds	1	–	3	1	4 Welsh – 1
2nd Colds. "	–	–	1	2	
7th. London	–	–	–	1	
6th London	1	–	–	–	
R.F.A Lond. Dn	–	–	1	–	
3rd Lond. R.E.	–	–	1	–	
Totals.	2	–	7	7	
Other Divs					To Light Duty
2nd Innis Fus.	1	–	–	1	2 Gren. Gds – 1
1st. Seaforths	–	–	–	2	5 Kings – 1
1st. Glouces.	–	–	–	1	RE – 1
2nd H.L.I.	–	–	–	2	1 Herts – 1
4th. Suffolks.	–	1	–	–	1 Kings – 3
2nd Bl. Watch.	–	1	–	–	1 R Berks – 1
2nd Oxfords.	–	–	–	2	1 K.R.R – 3
2nd R.W. Fus.	–	–	–	1	
1st. Northants.	–	1	–	–	
1st. Camerons.	–	–	–	1	
2nd S. Staffs.	1	–	–	–	
1st. L.N. Lancs.	–	1	–	–	
71st Punjabs att} 41st Dogras }	–	1	–	–	
2nd Sussex	–	1	–	–	
Totals	2	6	–	10	

Prevailing Disease – Nil.
Suffering with Dropsy Nil

Evac'd M.A.C.

Officers 37
Other Rks. 35

Ret'd duty
Officers Nil
Other Rks. 3

Ret'd Lt. Duty
Other Rks. 11.

		Sick	Wndd.
Admitted	Offrs.	4	6
	Other Rks.	7	17
Evac'd	Officers	–	37
	Other Rks.	14	35
Remaining	Officers	4	15
	Other Rks	17	77.

P.A. Lloyd Jones
Capt. RAMC
O.C. No. 4 Fd. Ambce.

No. 4 Fd. Ambce.

Nominal Roll of officers admitted during 24 hours ended 9 am. 11/5/15

Lt. Col.	C. A. WILDING,	2nd. Innis. Fus.	Injury R. Knee
Major.	P.B. SANGSTER,	Bde. Maj. Ferozepore Bde.	Myalgia
Capt.	C.F. NIXON,	7(?)th. Punjabs att. 41st. Dogras	G.S.W. L. Arm
Capt.	H.D. HILL	1st. L.N. Lancs.	" Back.
2nd Lt.	C.N. GREEN,	2nd. Sussex	" L Arm & Side
Capt.	C.C.S. MACLEOD	2nd Bl. Wch.	" Abdomen.
Lieut.	A. H. SUTHERLAND	- do -	" Legs.
2nd Lt.	I. B. MUIRHEAD	6th London	N.Y.D.
Lieut.	A de HAMELL,	2nd. S. Staffs	Injury R. Leg.
2nd Lt.	K.E. MONRO	1st Northants	G.S.W. Legs, Arms & Buttocks.

P.A. Lloyd Jones
Capt. RAMC.
OC. No. 4 "Fd." Ambce.

ADMS
11/5/15

No. 4 Field Ambce.

Evacuation Return. 9 a.m.

Officers - Lying - 11
Sitting - 2.

Other Ranks Lying - 30
Sitting - 4

P H Lloyd Jones
Capt.
~~Lt.~~ RAMC.
~~for~~ O.C. No. 4 Fd. Ambce.

O.C. No 7. MAC.
11/5/15.

No. 4 Field Ambulance

No. of sick and wounded, by Units, admitted during 24 hours ended 9am. 12/5/15

Units - 47th Lond. Div.	Officers Sick	Officers wndd	Other Rks Sick	Other Rks wndd	
15th. London			-	1	To duty
21st. London			-	2	
2nd Gren: Gds.			1	2	1 S. Staffs.
2nd Colds. Gds.			-	1	To light duty
3rd Colds Gds.			4	-	
1st. Irish Gds.			2	-	1 2nd R.W.F.
1st. Herts.				1	1 2nd G. Gds.
London Dn Am. Col.			1	-	1 31st Co. R.E.
E. A. R. E.			2	-	1 4th. R.W.F.
London Supply Col.			1	-	
Total.			11	7	
Other Divs.					
2nd Wilts.			1	1	
8th. R. Scots.			4	-	
2nd Warwicks			8	-	
R. W. Fus.			3	-	
2nd Welsh att 170 Co. R.E.			1	3	
2nd Queens			6	-	
5th Worces			1	-	
1st. Camerons			1	-	
2nd Oxfords	-	1	-	-	
2nd Bedfords.			-	2	
1st. Gloucesters.	1	-	-	-	
Army Ordnance Dept.	1	-	-	-	
2nd. Dn A. Col.	-	-	1	-	
A.S.C. 350th Co.	1	-	-	-	
2nd R. Scots. Fusrs.	1	-	-	-	
RAMC att 2. R. Mun. Fus.	1	-	-	-	
Total.	5	1	26	6	

Evac'd by M.A.C.

Officers. 11
Other Rks. 44

Ret'd duty

Officers Nil
Other Rks. 1

Ret'd Lt. duty

Other Rks. 4

Prevailing Disease - Nil
Suffering with Dropsy - Nil.

		Sick	wnd.
Admitted	Officers	5	1
"	Other Rks.	37	13
Evac'd	Officers	4	7
"	Other Rks.	43	54
Remaining	Officers	6	4
"	Other Rks.	47	53

Major G. de S. Dudley, Army Ordnance Dept. Fracture Ribs.
2nd Lt. R. E. Trevithick 350th Co: A.S.C. Appendicitis
Lieut. F. W. Ollis 1st. Gloucesters. Exostosis Tibia
2nd Lt. C. B. Baker, 2nd Oxfords, G.S.W. R. Shdr.
Lieut. J. E. Gilks, 2nd R. Scots Fus. Synovitis.
" A. F. Wright, RAMC att 2. R.M.F. Influenza.,

R. A. L. [illegible]
Capt. RAMC.
O.C. No. 4 F.A.

No. 4 Field Ambulance.

Evacuation Return – 9am. 12/5/15.

Officers Lying. } Nil.
Sitting. }

Other Rks. Lying. 8
Sitting. 4.

A. G. H. Lovell

Capt. RAMC
OC. No. 4 Fd. Ambce.

O.C. No 7 MAC.

Army Form C. 2118.

Instructions regarding War Diaries and Intelligence Summaries are contained in F. S. Regs., Part II. and the Staff Manual respectively. Title pages will be prepared in manuscript.

WAR DIARY
or
~~INTELLIGENCE SUMMARY.~~
(Erase heading not required.)

Hour, Date, Place	Summary of Events and Information	Remarks and references to Appendices
13th May, 1915 BETHUNE.	Number of Casualties. 41 Evacuated by M.A.C. Officers 4 Other Rks. 25 The following officers died from wounds received in action Capt G. C. S. MacLeod, 2nd Black Watch. Lieut J.H.B. Fletcher, 7th London 2nd Lt. L.C.A. Squire — do — Capt. W.D. Hill, 1st L.N. Lancs. The following men arrived for duty from Base Details Rouen:- No. 43094 Pte Toon W.T. RAMC 42989 " Thompson V. " 43180 " Turner G. " 43588 " Turner H. "	PAG

(73989) W4141—463. 400,000. 9/14. H.&J.Ltd. Forms/C. 2118/10.

No. 1 Field Ambce.

No. of sick and wounded officers admitted during the week ended 9 a.m. 31/5/15.

Corps or Unit	Officers		Other Ranks		
	Sick	Wounded	Sick	Wounded	
1st Indian Bde			3		[illegible]
2nd Inf. Bde			1		Transferred
	–	–	4	–	

[illegible]

Capt. R.A.M.C.
O.C. No. 1 Field Ambce.

31/5/15

No. 4 Field Ambulance.

Numbers of sick & wounded admitted, by Units, during 24 hours ended 9 am. 13/5/15

Unit. 2nd Divn.	Officers Sick	Officers Wnd.	Other Rks Sick	Other Rks Wnd.	Remarks.
2nd Gren. Gds.			2	-	
2nd Colds Gds.			1	3	
3rd Colds. Gds.			3	2	
1st. Irish "			4		
1st. Herts.			3		
1st. R. Berks.			7		
1st Kings.	1			1	
1st. K.R.R.			1		
1st. S.A.R.E.			1		
170th Co. R.E.			1		
2nd Oxfords.	1				
Total.	2	–	23	6	
Other Divs.					
6th N. Yorks.				2	
2nd Yorks.				2	
2nd R. Scots Fus.			1		
2nd Bedfords.			3		
4th R.W.F.	1				
18th Lon. Irish.	1				
2nd R.M. Fus.			1	1	
8th London				1	
1st Glouces.				3	
2nd Welsh				1	
7th London		2			
R.G.A. 6th T.M. Bat.			2		
" 9th Sge. Bat.			1		
A.S.C. 6th. Divn.			1		
R.G.A. 11th Sge Bat.		1			
20th London	1				
R.A.M.C.	1				
	4	3	9	10	

Prevailing Disease Influenza
No admitted with Dropsy 1.

Evac'd by M.A.C.
- Officers – 10.
- Other Rks. 32

Retd Duty
- Officers Nil
- Other Rks. Nil

Retd Lt. Duty
- Officers Nil
- Other Rks. Nil

		Sick	Wnd.
Admitted	Officers.	6	3
"	Other Rks.	32	16
Evac'd	Officers	6	4
"	Other Rks.	14	18
Remg	Officers	4	1
"	Other Rks.	60	49

List of officers admitted see following page.

P. A. Lloyd Jones
Capt. RAMC
OC. No 4 FA.

ADMS. 2nd Divn.
" " 13/5/15.

Officers admitted 24 hrs ended 9 a.m. 13/5/15.

Lieut C.A. FOWKE, 2nd Oxfords, N.Y.D.
2nd Lt. T. CLAYTON, 4th R.W.F. Acute Urticaria.
Major T.W. SHEPPARD 1st. Kings Neurasthenia
2nd Lt. C.T. STABB, 18th Lond. Irish N.Y.D.
Lt. Col A.B. HUBBACK, 20th Lond. Jaundice
Lieut. H.W. POWELL, RAMC Diarrhoea
2nd Lt. L.C.H. SQUIRE, 7th London G.S.W. Neck.
Lieut J.H.V. FLETCHER, —do— " Legs & Testicles
Lieut R.M. CHADWICK, R.G.A., 115 Sge Batt. Sh. Wnd {Head Arms & Leg

P.H. Lloyd Jones.
Capt. RAMC
O.C. No 4 Fd. Ambce.

ADMS, 2nd Divn

No. 4 Field Ambulance.

Evacuation Return 9am. 13/5/15.

Officers -	Lying	—
	Sitting	—
Other Rks -	Lying	4
	Sitting.	1.

P.A. Lloyd Jones.

Lieut. RAMC.
for O.C. No. 4 Fd. Ambce.

O.C. No. 7 M.A.C.

Instructions regarding War Diaries and Intelligence Summaries are contained in F. S. Regs., Part II. and the Staff Manual respectively. Title pages will be prepared in manuscript.

WAR DIARY
or
~~INTELLIGENCE SUMMARY.~~
(*Erase heading not required.*)

Army Form C. 2118.

Hour, Date, Place	Summary of Events and Information	Remarks and references to Appendices
14th May, 1915. BETHUNE.	The following Secret orders were received from ADMS. 2nd Divn "C Bearer Sub. Divn 47 A. O.C. 47 A. DADMS C " " " 57 A. " 57 A. C " " " 67 A. " 67 A. G. Staff for information M. 143. 14 N. B. X. Moves not to take place until definite orders received Situation at present moment. No. 47 A. Tent Divn open at Com. Hopital - 250 beds. one Ambce Motor Car. X B. bearer Sub. Divn to move to LOCON in reserve. 2 Ambce cars 3 horse ambces. C bearer Sub. Divn with 4th Gds Bde. at X 8 b 4 Ambce Cars. 57 A. Tent Divn and A bearer Sub. Divn at LOCON in reserve B. bearer Sub. Divn at X 16 a Divnl Collecting Station 3 cars, 6 horse ambces. C bearer Sub. Divn with 5th Bde. at S 2 c 4 ambce cars. 67 A. Tent Divn and A bearer Sub. Divn open at Sem. St. Vaast - 800 beds. one ambce car, X B bearer Sub. Divn to move to LOCON in reserve 2 cars. C bearer Sub. Divn with 6th. Bde. at X 12 a 4 cars. Adv. 2. Divn 3 pm. (Signed) M. P. Holt. Col ADMS.	PHG

(73989) W4141—463. 400,000. 9/14. H.&J.Ltd. Forms/C. 2118/10.

Army Form C. 2118.

Instructions regarding War Diaries and Intelligence Summaries are contained in F. S. Regs., Part II. and the Staff Manual respectively. Title pages will be prepared in manuscript.

WAR DIARY
or
~~INTELLIGENCE~~ SUMMARY.

(Erase heading not required.)

Hour, Date, Place	Summary of Events and Information	Remarks and references to Appendices
14th May, 1915. BETHUNE (Continued).	The Commanding Officer went to Lillers and procured Medical Stores for 1000 patients and made arrangements for 2000 blankets to be supplied. Number of Casualties:- 53. Evacuated by No 7 M.A.C. Officers - 5. Other Rks. 39. Lieut H. Mc H. McCullagh, RAMC (S.R.) promoted to Captain (S.R.).	PAG

(73989). W4141—463. 400,000. 9/14. H.&J.Ltd. Forms/C. 2118/10.

No. 4 Field Ambulance.

Numbers of Sick and Wounded, by Units, admitted during 24 hours ended 9 a.m. 14/5/15.

Unit – 2nd Divn.	Officers Sick	Officers Wnd.	Other Ranks Sick	Other Ranks Wnd.	Remarks.
2nd Grenadier Gds.			1	11	Officers to Duty
2nd H.L.I.					
2nd Oxfords		1		4	Lt. C. A. Fooke 2nd Oxfords.
2nd Innisk. Fus.				4	
2nd Worcesters					
7th Kings.			1		
9th Kings		1			
R.F.A. 41st Bde.		1			
1st Irish Gds.	1				
Total.	1	3	2	19	
Other Divns.					
1st Glosters.		1		1	
6th W. Yorks				4	
4th R.W.F.				1	
1st Scots Gds.			1		
4th R. H'drs.			1		
6th London	1			1	
R.F.A. 58th Batt.			1		
R.F.A. 29th B.A.C.	1				
R.H.A. V. Batt.		1		1	
A.S.C. 3rd Co.			1		
R.E. 3 Lond. Fd. Co.		1			
Total.	2	3	4	7	

Prevailing Disease Nil.
Admitted to Div Rest Stn Nil

Evac. M.A.C.
Officers. 4
Other Rks. 25

To Duty
Officers 1
Other Rks. –

To Light Duty
Other Ranks. –

To Barges
Officers –
Other Rks. 5

		Sick	Wound.
Admitted	Officers	3	6
"	Other Rks.	6	26
Evac'd	Officers	3	2
"	Other Rks.	18	12
Remaining	Officers	6	4
"	Other Rks.	48	63

P. A. Lloyd Jones
Capt. RAMC
OC. No. 4 Fd. Ambce.

ADMS. 2nd Divn.
14/5/15.

No. 4 Field Ambulance.

Officers admitted No. 4 Fd. Ambce. 24 hrs. ended 9 am. 14/5/15.

2nd Lt. E. PAYNE, 9th Kings G.S.W. L. Shdr.
Capt. R. E. F. WEMYSS 2 Q.B.A.C. R.F.A. Hernia.
2nd Lt. C. E. WAUHOPE Wes. Bde R.F.A. Sh. Wnd Hands R. Thigh
Lieut. Hon. N. F. SOMERSET, 1st. Gloucs. Wound Concussion.
" C. A. FOWKE 2nd Oxfords. Sh. Wnd R. Hand.
" W. S. WINGATE-GRAY R.H.A. V Batt. Sh. Wnd Head.
" W. H. HILLYER, R.E. 3rd Lond. F. Co. " " Head (Slight)
Rev. Fr. GWYNN, att. 1st Irish Gds. Myalgia
2nd Lt. J. E. GREGORY, 6th London. Influenza.

P. H. Lloyd Jones

Capt. RAMC.
OC. No. 4 Fd. Ambce.

A.D.M.S. 2nd Divn

No. 4 Fd. Ambce.

Evacuation Return 9am. 14/5/15.

Officers - Lying - } Nil.
Sitting - }

Other Ranks - Lying - 8.
Sitting - 7.

P.A. [illegible]

Capt ~~[illegible]~~ RAMC.
~~for~~ O.C. No. 4 Fd. Ambce.

O.C. No. 7 M.A.C.

No 4. Field Ambulance

Evacuation Return 3/pm

Officers Lying: 2 / Sitting: 2 } 4 Servants

Other Ranks. Lying: 4 / Sitting: 13

O.C. No 7 Motor Convoy.
14 - 5 - 15

Lieut RAMC
for O.C. No 4 Field Amb

Instructions regarding War Diaries and Intelligence Summaries are contained in F. S. Regs., Part II. and the Staff Manual respectively. Title pages will be prepared in manuscript.

WAR DIARY
or
INTELLIGENCE SUMMARY.

(*Erase heading not required.*)

Army Form C. 2118.

Hour, Date, Place	Summary of Events and Information	Remarks and references to Appendices
15th. May, 1915. BETHUNE.	Capt. W. Mc. H. Mc. Cullagh, RAMC (S.R.) assumed command of C Section Bearer Sub. Division, at X 86, with 4th (Guards) Infty. Brigade. The following orders received from ADMS. 2nd Divn. " OC. 4 7.A., OC. 5 7.A., OC. 6 7.A., DADMS., GS. for information. M 144 15 1. B bearer Sub. Divn 47.A. with 2 Ambce cars and 3 horse Ambces. will move to LOCON - report to DADMS. by midnight and await orders. 2. B. bearer Sub-Divn 67.A. with one ambce. car will move to LOCON report to DADMS there by midnight and await orders. 3. One ambce car with aid post detachment of 67A. will remain at Advanced H.Q. at disposal of ADMS. 4. ADMS. 1st. Divn has offered to assist by sending spare motor ambces. to LOCON. These will arrive there about 4 a.m. tomorrow. Probably 15 in number. 5. Capt. TAYLOR will regulate movements of all ambce. cars at LOCON. Adv. H.Q. 8.10 p.m. (Signed) M. A. Holt. Col. ADMS." One complete Bearer Sub Division was sent to Capt. Mc. Cullagh.	PHG

(73989) W4141—463. 400,000. 9/14. H.&J.Ltd. Forms/C. 2118/10.

Army Form C. 2118.

Instructions regarding War Diaries and Intelligence Summaries are contained in F. S. Regs., Part II. and the Staff Manual respectively. Title pages will be prepared in manuscript.

WAR DIARY
or
INTELLIGENCE SUMMARY

(Erase heading not required.)

Hour, Date, Place	Summary of Events and Information	Remarks and references to Appendices

Forms/C. 2118/10.

No. 4 Field Ambulance.

No. of sick & wounded, by Units, admitted during 24 hours ended 9 am. 15/5/15.

Unit – 2nd Divn	Officers Sick	Officers Wnd.	Other Rks. Sick	Other Rks. Wnd.
2nd Grenadier Gds.	–	–	3	–
1st Irish Gds.	–	–	2	–
2nd Oxfords	–	–	3	–
R.A.M.C. att. 2. Oxfds.	–	–	1	–
1st. K.R.R.	–	1	1	4
2nd H.L.I.	–	1	–	5
7th. Kings.	–	1	–	–
2nd Innis Fus.	–	2	1	5
2nd Worces.	–	–	–	2
1st. R. Berks	–	–	–	1
R.G.A. 1st. Sge Batt.	–	1	–	–
Total.	–	6	11	17
Other Divns.				
London Scott.	–	–	2	1
15th. London	–	1	–	
17th "	–	–	–	1
7th "	–	–	–	2
2nd "	–	–	–	1
2nd Yorks	–	–	–	2
4th Camerons	1	–	–	–
2nd Leicesters	–	–	–	1
R.H.A. X Batt.	–	–	–	1
A.S.C. Lond. Div	–	–	2	–
R.F.A. 44 Bde	–	–	2	–
22nd London.	1	–	–	1
R.H.A. – C.R.A. Staff 2nd Indian Cav. Div.	–	–	–	
Total.	2	1	6	10

To Duty

2nd Bedfds – 2.
8th R. Scots – 5.
2 Wilts – 2.
2 Warwks – 3.
R.W.F. – 1
2 Queens – 1
14

To Light Duty

3 Coldm. Gds. 1.
6 T.B. R.G.A. 1.
1 R. Berks 1.
1 Herts 1.
170 Co R.E. 1.
1 Irish Gd. 2.
7

Prevailing disease Nil.
Admitted with Dropsy – 1.

		Sick	Wnd.
Admitted	Officers	2	7
"	Other Rks.	17	27
Evac'd	Officers	2	3
"	Other Rks.	41	40
Remaining	Officers	6	7
"	Other Rks.	24	45

Evac'd by M.A.C.
Officers 5
Other Rks. 39

Evac'd to Barge
Other Rks. – 12

Trans. 22nd Fd. Amb.
Other Rks – 9

To Duty
Other Rks. 14

To Light Duty
Other Rks. 7.

R.A. Lloyd Jones
Capt. R.A.M.C.
O.C. No. 4 Fd. Amb.

A.D.M.S. 2nd Divn.

No. 4 Fd. Ambce.

Roll of Officers admitted.

2nd Lieut B. SCOTT, 15th London, Shell wnd Scalp.
Lieut H.G.A. ALEXANDER, 7th Kings " " Knee.
2nd Lt. L.F. TAYLOR, 1st K.R.R. " " Shoulder
" " C.C. MYLLES, 2nd H.L.I. " " L. Hand
" " D.C.G. DAVIES, R.G.A. (1st Sge Batt) " " {Head, Arm, Chest, Legs
" " J. BLAKENEY, 2nd R. Innis. Fus. " " Face.
" " V.E.S. MATTOCKS, —do— " " R. Shoulder.
MAJOR J. LOCKIE, 4th Camerons, N.Y.D.
Capt. L. BOOSEY, 22nd London, N.Y.D.

P. A. Lloyd Jones
Capt. RAMC
OC. No. 4 Fd. Ambce.

A.D.M.S. 2nd Div.
15/5/15.

No. 4 Field Ambulance.

Evacuation Return, 5/5/15 - 9 am.

Officers - Lying } Nil.
Sitting. }

Other Rks Lying —
Sitting 8.

P. A. Lloyd Jones.
~~Lieut.~~ Capt. RAMC
~~for~~ OC. No 4 ~~Fd~~ Amb.

OC. No 7. MAC.

15/5/15.

Army Form C. 2118.

Instructions regarding War Diaries and Intelligence Summaries are contained in F. S. Regs., Part II. and the Staff Manual respectively. Title pages will be prepared in manuscript.

WAR DIARY

or

~~INTELLIGENCE SUMMARY.~~

(Erase heading not required.)

Hour, Date, Place	Summary of Events and Information	Remarks and references to Appendices
16th May, 1915 BETHUNE	Large number of wounded admitted from early this morning as a result of the attack by the combined 2nd and 7th Divns. The first casualties were admitted at about 3am. and continued to arrive in large numbers during the 24 hours and in not so great numbers during the following day. At one time The Hospital was so full that cases could not be ~~[struck out]~~ dressed for some time after arrival ~~[struck out]~~ + were placed temporarily under the trees in the grounds. At about 5pm. the ADMS 2nd Divn ordered 40 lying down cases to be transferred to No. 2 Fd Ambce to relieve the pressure of work. (PHG)	
	So that my Medical Officers might get some rest 4 Medical Officers of other Units were lent to us for the night. Evacuation to the M.A.C. cars and also to the Ambulance Barges was continuous throughout the day and up till midnight.	PHG.
	The Director General visited the Dressing Station.	
	H.R.H. The Prince of Wales visited the Officers' Dressing Station.	
	Casualties admitted numbered - Officers 119. Other Rks. 398.	
	Evacuations by No 7. M.A.C. Officers. 108 Other Rks. 270.	
	Evacuations to Barges - Officers 8 Other Rks. 14.	

No. 4 Field Ambulance.

Nos. of sick and wounded, by Units, admitted during 24 hours ended 9 a.m. 16/5/15.

Unit. 2nd Div.	Officers Sick	Officers Wnd	Other Rks. Sick	Other Rks. Wnd.
2nd Colds. Gds.	1	-	-	-
2nd Grenadier Gds.			1	
2nd Innis. Fus.		3	2	20
1st. K.R.R.		3		3
1st. Herts.			1	
1st. R. Berks.		2	6	11
2nd Worces.		1		7
2nd H.L.I.		1		
9th. H.L.I.		2		4
5th. K.R.R.				1
1st. Kings	1	1		2
2nd Oxfords.		1		1
R.E. 31. Co.			2	1
" 2. Sig. Co.		1		1
" 11 Fd. Co.				
R.G.A. 1st. Siege Batt.				3
R.F.A. 17 Batt.			1	
R.G.A. 7 Mtn. Batt.	1			
2nd S. Staffs.				1
7th. Kings.		2		
R.E. East. Ang.			3	
Total.	3	17	16	56
Other Divs				
2nd R. Sussex.				1
5th London				1
R.A.M.C. (2nd Queens.)		1		
1. E. Surrey (att 2. Wks.)	1			
19 London	1	+		
2nd Bedfords.		1		
R.F.A. West Rdg. Bde.				1
" 44 Bde.			1	
R.H.A. T. Batt.		1		
R.F.A. 54 Batt.		1		
R.F.A. 6 Lond. Bde.	1			
Total	3	4	1	3

Light Duty

1 Irish Gds 1
1 Kings 1
1 Berks 2
2 Worces. 2
1 Herts 1
2. G. Gds. 1
2 Innis. 1
9

One German admitted wnded.

Prevailing Disease Nil
admitted with Nephritis - 1

Evac'd M.A.C.

Officers - 10
Other Rks. 39

To Barge

Officers 3
Other Rks. 5

To Lt. Duty

Officers -
Other Rks. 9

		Sick	Wnd
Admitted	Officers	6	21
"	Other Rks.	17	59
Evac'd	Officers.	4	6
"	Other Rks.	11	38
Remaining.	Officers	8	22
"	Other Rks.	20	102

Officers admitted -

2nd Lt. D.N. Morgan 7th. Batt. [illegible] G.A. Neurasthenia
Capt. F.S. Montague-Bates ✓ 1st. E. Surrey att. 2 Hawks. Diarrhoea
2nd Lt. H.H. Burn 2nd Colds. Guards Tonsillitis
" " W.F. Rogers R.H.A. T. Batt. Shell wnd Head
Lt. Col. J. MacHaugh, 19th. Lond. N.Y.D.
Lieut. J.R. Hope, 1st. Kings N.Y.D.
" G.H. Fisher 1st. K.R.R. Scalp Wound
" F.R.P. Curry, 54th Batt. R.F.A. Shock.
2nd Lt. J.E. Mc Intosh ✓ 2nd H.L.I. Shell wnd L. Leg.
Lieut. A. Trewby ✓ R.E. 11th Fd. Co. G.S.W. L. Butt. + Abdomen
Lieut. E. Basden ✓ 1st. R. Berks. " R. Side
" J.S. Alston ✓ 1st. K.R.R. " L. Arm.
Capt. R.C. Smythe ✓ 2nd Innis. Fus. " R. Shdr.
" G. Steward ✓ " " " " L. Chest.
Lieut. N.H. Stewart ✓ R.A.M.C. (att. 2. Queens) B.W. L. Leg.
Capt. E.M. Allfrey ✓ 1st. R. Berks. G.S.W. R. Hand.
Lieut. G.W. Miller ✓ 1st. Kings. Shell W. L. Side
" C.S. Barnes ✓ 2nd Oxf. Bs. " " Arms + Legs.
2nd Lt. E.E.J. Moore ✓ 2nd Innis Fus. G.S.W. R. Wrist
" " A.C. Murray ✓ 9th. H.L.I. Shell wnd L. Arm
Capt. J.S. Dean ✓ 7th. Kings. G.S.W. R. Leg + Finger
2nd Lt. B. Temple ✓ 2nd Worcesters. " L. Thigh
" " L.W. Roper ✓ 7th. Kings Contusion Head
Capt. F.L. Pardoe ✓ D.S.O. 1st K.R.R. Shell wnd Back
" C.C. Hewitt ✓ 2nd. Innis Fus. G.S.W. L. Arm
2nd Lt. J.A. Robertson ✓ 9th. H.L.I. Shell wnd L. Arm + Hip.
Capt. G. de C. Glover ✓ 2. S. Staffs. " " Head
2nd Lt. R.A.B. Orlebar ✓ 2nd Bedfords. G.S.W. L. Shdr.

P. A. Lloyd Jones
Capt. RAMC
O.C. No 4 Fd Amb

Instructions regarding War Diaries and Intelligence Summaries are contained in F. S. Regs., Part II. and the Staff Manual respectively. Title pages will be prepared in manuscript.

WAR DIARY
or
~~INTELLIGENCE~~ SUMMARY.
(Erase heading not required.)

Army Form C. 2118.

Hour, Date, Place	Summary of Events and Information	Remarks and references to Appendices
17th. May, 1915. BETHUNE.	Casualties admitted during the day were again very numerous, but not so heavy as the previous day. The Director General visited the Dressing Station and H.R.H. the Prince of Wales again visited the Officers' Dressing Station. 2 Medical Officers were lent to us for the night to assist in the dressing of cases. Number of casualties – Officers 51. Other Rks. 189. Evacuated by No 7 M.A.C. – Officers 61. Other Rks. 241.	PRG

(73989) W4141—463. 400,000. 9/14. H.&J.Ltd. Forms/C. 2118/10.

No 4 Field Ambulance

No. of sick and wounded admitted during 24 hours ended 9 am. 17/5/15

2nd Divⁿ Units.	Officers. Sick	Officers. Wndd.	Other Rks. Sick	Other Rks. Wndd.
2nd Inniskg. Fus.		5		36
2nd Oxfords.		9		36
2nd S. Staffs.		5		37
1st. Kings.		1		22
1st. R. Berks.				19
2nd H. L. I.		2		20
9th. H. L. I.		2		14
2nd Worces.		2		22
5th Kings.		11		19
7th. Kings.		2		13
R.E. 5th. Fd. Co.		1		1
1st. Irish Gds.				6
1st. K. R. R.		7		17
2nd Gren. Gds.				4
~~3rd Kings~~				
R.E. 11th. Fd. Co.		1		3
1st. Herts.				5
R. G. A. 7th Mtn. Batt.		1		1
" 1st. Sge Batt.				1
" 6th. Trench "	1	[illegible]		
~~2nd Gren. Gds.~~				
Total.	1	49	–	276
Other Divs				
2nd Scots Guards.				11
2nd Border Regt.		3		17
2nd Queens.		6		15
1st. R. I. F.		5		13
2nd Warwicks.		3		11
2nd Gordons		8		12
17th London				2
3rd S. Staffs.				2
3rd Kings.				1
1st. Gren. Gds.		1		3
8th R. Scots.		5		10
2nd Bedfords.				4
6th. Gordons.		3		2
1st. S. Staffs.		3		1
2nd R Scots Fus.				4
3rd Oxfords.				1
2nd Leicesters				1
R. G. A. 10 Sge Batt.				1
R.E. 7th Sig Co.				1
Forward	–	37	–	112

Other Div. Units.	Officers Sick	Officers Wndd.	Other Rks. Sick	Other Rks. Wndd.
	1	31	–	117
R.F.A. 113 Batt.				
RAMC. att. (1 R.W.F.)		1		
8th London		3		
16th Cav. I.A (att 1. Gren Gds)		1		
3rd Northants		1		
19th London	1			
7th London		2		
1 L.N. Lancs (att 2 Bdfds)		1		
3 R.W.F. (att 1 R.W.F.)		1		
3. E. Surrey (att 1 S. Staffs)		1		
3 Seaforths (att 2 Gordons)		1		
Chaplain 22 Bde.		1		
3 R.W.F. (att. 2. Queens)		1		
8th H.L.I. (att. 8 R Scots)		1		
~~1st Gren Gds~~				
Buffs (att Queens)		1		
2nd Yorks.		1		
3rd Northants. (att. R.W.F.)		1		
1st London Irish		1		
R.G.A. 6th Sge Batt.		1		
R.F.A. 105 Batt.		2		
" 71st "		1		
" 54th "	1	1		
R.G.A. 81 Sge Batt.		1		
R.F.A. 60th Batt.		1		
" 35th "		1		
R.E. Highland Co.		1		
R.G.A. 115 Sge Batt		1		
Germans.		2		9
	2	68 ~~117~~	–	122

Evac'd M.A.C.
Officers 108
Other Rks. ~~[illegible]~~ 270
Duty
Officers –
Other Rks. –
Light Duty
Other Rks. 9
To Barges.
Officers 8
Other Rks 14

Lists of officers will follow.

		Sick	Wndd
Admitted	Officers	2	117
"	Other Rks.	–	398
Evac'd	Officers	2	117
"	Other Rks.	13	271
Remaing.	Officers	–	51
"	Other Rks.	27	177

P. A. Lloyd Jones.
Capt. RAMC
O.C. No. 4 Fd. Ambce.

A.D.M.S. 2nd Divn.

Roll of Officers admitted No 4 Fd. Ambce

24 hrs. ended 9 am. 17/5/15.

Capt. H. S. Blockley,	2nd Sth. Staffs.,	G.S.W. R. Arm
2nd Lt. R. A. F. Whistler	2nd. H. L. I.	" L. Hand
Capt. H. L. Bonham-Carter,	1st. K.R.R.,	Multiple small wounds
2nd Lt. H. B. Cox,	5th. Kings.	Shell wnd Hip & R. Leg.
Capt. J. H. Grindley	" "	" " Chin
" G. Blewitt	2nd Oxfords.	G.S.W. L. Shoulder
2nd Lt. W. L. Barnard,	"	" R. "
" " S. F. Johnson,	2nd Border	" L. Arm
Capt. H. M. Dillon	2nd Oxfords	" Buttocks
Major G. F. H. Dickson	1st R. W. F.	Shell wnd both Thighs
2nd Lt. J. Brammer	9th Royal Scots.	" " Wrist
" F. N. Goad	R.F.A. 7th M. B.	" " L. Hand & Thigh
" M. C. Lawrence	9th City of London	G.S.W. L. Hand
Lt. W. F. Chapman	1st R. W. F.	Shell wnd Left knee joint Frac. R. Femur
2nd Lt. D. Humphrey	2nd Queens	G.S.W. abdomen
Lt. R. H. Marshall	3rd N. Hants attd 1st N. Hants	Gastritis
Major A. C. H. Kennard	19th London	Colic
Lt. W. J. Graham	2nd London [illegible]	Shell wnd R. Hand
2nd Lt. G. Giles	-do-	" " L. Arm
" J. Thomson	-do-	" " R. Arm
Lt. R. A. Barrow	1st K.R.R.	" " R. Hand & Shdr
2nd Lt. C. J. Hart	2nd Worcesters	G.S.W. R. Arm
Capt. L. M. Lloyd Mostyn	1st R. W. F.	" Back
" J. A. Evans	7th Kings	Shell wnd R. Arm & Thigh
2nd Lt. G. P. Lindsay	2nd Borders.	" " Buttock
Major C. W. Scott	71st Bty. R.F.A.	" " Face & Arm
Lieut. C. W. Evans	1st South Staffs	Shell " L. Hip & Arm

Capt. F. J. N. Savage Armstrong 1st South Staffs. G.S.W. L. Hand
Lt. L. S. P. Davidson 6th Gordon Hdrs Shell Wnd R. Shoulder
Capt Tolson 2nd Ox & Bucks " , R. Leg
" K. H. Crawford 2nd Innis. Fus. G.S.W. Back
Lt. F. R. Curry 54th Bty R.F.A. Wound (Concussion)
Lt. C. E. W. Charrington 2nd South Staffs. G.S.W. L. Arm
2nd Lt. H. O'N. de H. Segrave 2nd Warwicks " L. Arm
" V. G. Hallam 2nd South Staffs. Shell Wnd Forehead
Lt. H. F. Gannons Williams 1st R.W.F. G.S.W. L. Leg
" A. M. Mackay 9th H. L. I. Contused Wnd Thigh
2nd Lt. A. E. Dent 1st K. R. R. G.S.W. Hand & Leg
Major H. D. Barnes 7th London " Chest
2nd Lt. W. E. Mumford 7th Kings Shell Wnd L. Shoulder
" B. Whitehouse L. N. Lancs attd. 2nd Bedfds. " " Face.
" W. E. Hamblin 5th Coy. R.E. Scalp Wound.
" W. I. G. Farren 3rd R.W.F. attch 1st R.W.F. G.S.W. R. Leg.
Lt. F. M. Coly 3rd East Surrey attd 1st S. Staffs. Shell Wnd L. Side
2nd Lt. L. F. Garratt R.G.A. 6 Trench Bty. N.Y.D (Sick)
Capt. W. B. J. Reid 3rd Seaforths attd. 2 Gordons Wnd Ankle Frac. Elbow
" The Rev. M. Peel Chaplain 22nd Bde Shell Wnd Thigh, Scalp & Neck
2nd Lt. R. D. Cochrane 8th London " " R. Eye.
" A. Blair 8th Royal Scots. G.S.W. L. Shoulder
Capt R. J. Fairclough 5th Kings L'pool Shell Wnd L. Arm Fract.
2nd G. F. Richardson 5th -do- " " L. Calf & R. Ankle
Major S. S. G. Ahern 5th -do- G.S.W. L. Side
Lt E. T. Birkett 3rd R.W.F. attch. 2nd Queens Shell Wnd Face & Legs
" W. Kelsey R. AM C attch R.W.F. " " L. Arm
Capt D. R. Grindley Fry 5th King's L'pool G.S.W. Ankle
Lt. C. T. Holmes 2nd Warwicks " Thigh
Lt. D. W. Rowling 1st Kings L'pool " Forehead

Capt. S. F. Hammick   2nd Ox & Bucks   Contusion L. Foot
Major R. L. Haynes   R.G.A. 6th Seige Bty   Shell wnd R. Foot
Lt. J. M. Dickinson   16th Cav. I.A. attch 1st Gren. Gds   " " L. Arm
" G. W. Titherington   2nd Ox & Bucks   Shell wnd R. F'arm
√Major L. M. Bucknill   105th Bty R.F.A.   " " Spinal Column
Capt J. B. Bryne   81st Seige Bty R.G.A.   G.S.W. L. Leg
2nd Lt. J. B. Coates   2nd Queens   " L. Thigh
Lt. G. Duguid   2nd Gordon Hdrs   " R. Forearm
Capt L. A. Pauly   1st K.R.R.   " Both Eyes
" T. P. Croysdale   8th London   Shell wnd Face
" Garnier   2nd Queens   " " Frac. Humerus & Back
" J. Rawbotham   8th H.L.I. attch 8th R. Scots   " " Buttock
" S. Knox Gore   1st K.R.R.
Lt. W. Longbottom   5th Hamps   Shell wnd Scalp.
Capt W. E. Greig   - do -   G.S.W. Buttocks, Leg & Arms
Lt. R. B. Kerr   8th Royal Scots   Shell wnd R. Knee
" Hardy   1st K.R.R.   Fract. R. Femur
2Lt. C. R. Cross   11th Seige Bty R.G.A.   Wound Concussion
" W. R. Ellison   105th Bty R.F.A.   G.S.W. R. Buttock & Scalp
" R. H. F. Duckworth   R.E. 5th Field Coy.   " R. Arm
Lt. F. C. St. Aubyn   1st Gren. Gds.   Shell wnd Chest & Face
Major H. F. Kirkpatrick   The Buffs attch 2 Queens   G.S.W. Face
2nd Lt. A. G. MacNaughton   9th H.L.I.   Shell wnd L. Buttock & R. Eye
Lt. R. C. D. Owen   1st R.W.F.   G.S.W. L. Thigh
2nd Lt. J. C. Ludlow   2nd Innis Fus.   " R. Hip & Buttock
" C. S. Brownfield   6th Gordon Hdrs   " L. Leg
" A. Todd   2nd Yorks Lincs   " L. Arm
Capt G. Nelson   19th London   Shell wnd L. Hand
Lt. W. E. Wallace   8th R. Scots   Internal derangement L. Knee Joint

Lt. G. W. Phillimore	H.L.I.	G.S.W. Thigh & Head
Capt. C. T. Carfrae	R.F.A. 60th Bty.	G.S.W. Head
2 Lt. A.R. Wallis	7th Londons	Shell wnd Ear
" A.C. Lyons	2nd Inns Fus.	" " Face & Shoulder.
" R.G. Heinekey	2nd Queens	G.S.W. L. Breast.
Major J.A. Todd	8th Royal Scots.	
Capt. H.H. Tabler	2nd South Staffs	G.S.W. L. Elbow
2nd Lt. A.G. Prior	-do-	Shell wnd Scalp.
" F. J. Durnford	3rd N'Hants att 2.R.W.	G.S.W. Knee Jt.
" L. H. Tosswill	2nd Worces.	G.S.W. R. Elbow Fract.
" H.W. Deacon	35th Bty R.F.A.	" L. Elbow
Lt. E. H. Whitfield	2nd Ox & Bucks	Shell wnd Back & Head
" L. L. Hassell	1st South Staffs	Injury to Eye.
Capt. A. Buckley	5th Kings L'pool	Shell wnd R. Forearm
2nd Lt. J. H. Brookes	2nd Queens	" " Back
" A.G. Stevenson	2nd Gordons	G.S.W. Buttock
" J. Fairclough	2nd Queens	Comp. Fract. Ankle
Lt. H. Houston	London Irish	Shell wnd Calf & Knee
Capt. W.L. Evans	5th Kings L'pool	" " L. Leg
Lt. J.C.C. Thompson	2nd Inns Fus.	" " R. Shoulder
" F.A. Ledingham	7th Div. R.E.	G.S.W. L. Knee
2nd Lt. E.F. Carter	2nd Inns Fus.	" Thigh
Lt. C.C.D. Thompson	-do-	Shell wnd R. Arm
2nd Lt. D.H. Leak	2nd Border Regt	" " Temple
" D.A.A. Sewell	2nd Oxfords	" " Contus. Back.

Instructions regarding War Diaries and Intelligence Summaries are contained in F. S. Regs., Part II. and the Staff Manual respectively. Title pages will be prepared in manuscript.

WAR DIARY
or
~~INTELLIGENCE SUMMARY.~~
(Erase heading not required.)

Army Form C. 2118.

Hour, Date, Place	Summary of Events and Information	Remarks and references to Appendices
18th May, 1915 BETHUNE	The following is an extract from orders by Commanding Officer. "Officers are not to be put into the French Ward. The ward near the main entrance on the Ground Floor is to be used as an overflow ward for officers. Should it be considered dangerous in the opinion of the medical officer to transport a wounded officer after operation to the Officers' Dressing Station, he should be put into the overflow ward." Four medical officers were lent to us to carry on the work of dressings &c. during the night. Number of casualties - Officers - 48 Other Rks. 206. Evacuated by M.A.C. Officers 53. Other Rks. 173. The undermentioned men having arrived for duty from Base Details were taken on the strength. 43680 Pte Matthews T. RAMC 46672 " McAvoy W. " 43043 " Miller R. " 43664 " Mitchell W. " 43670 " McCleary W. " 49359 " Carnford L. "	PHG

(73989) W4141—463. 400,000. 9/14. H.&J.Ltd. Forms/C. 2118/10.

No. 4 Field Ambce

No. of sick and wounded, by Units, admitted during 24 hours ended 9 am. 18/5/15

Unit - 2nd Divn	Officers Sick	Officers wnd	Other Rks Sick	Other Rks wnd
2nd Grenadier Gds.		1✓		2
1st. Irish Gds.		1✓		1
1st. Herts.		1✓		-
1st. Kings.	1✓			30
1st. K.R.R.		1✓		7
2nd H.L.I.		3✓		22
9th H.L.I.			1	12
2nd Oxfords.		2✓		17
2nd S. Staffs.		2✓		35
7th. Kings.				4
1st. R. Berks.				13
2nd Innis Fus.				10
5th. Kings.				2
R.G.A. T.M. Batt.				1
A.O.C. att. 41 Bde R.F.A.				1
R.E. 11th. Fd. Co.		1✓		
2nd Worcesters.				10
Ind. Army att. 1st. R. Berks.		1✓		
5th. Warwicks att 170 Co R.E.		1✓		
N. Staffs att. 2. S. Staffs.		1✓		
Total	1	15	1	16/6
Other Divns.				
2nd Border.		4✓		1
1st. R.W.F.		2✓		
R.G.A 13 Sge Batt.		1✓		
2nd Gordons.		1✓		
2nd R. Scots att 8th.		1✓		
R.F.A 12. Batt.		1✓		1
2nd R. Scots		1✓		2
2nd London		1		
2nd Wilts.		1✓		
8th. R. Scots. ✓		2✓		
R.F.A 51st. Batt		1✓		
7th. London		1✓		
1st. S. Staffs.		2✓		
4th Camerons		5✓		1
24 London		2✓		
8 Gurkhas		1✓		
2nd Bedfords.		2✓		
R.A.M.C. att. 2nd Bedfds.		1✓		
" " 2. R. Scots.		1✓		
6th London		1✓		
3rd London				1
3rd Oxfords				1
1st. Gren. Gds.				1
2nd Scots -				1
2nd Bl. Watch.				2
13th R. Highlanders				1
R.F.A. 54th Batt.				1
8th H.L.I.				1
Germans / 1st Coldm. Gds.	1	1✓		8
2nd Queens				
13 R. Highd. Canadians				
	41	34		22

To Lt. Duty.

2. H.L.I.	1.
2 Oxfds.	7.
2 Worcs.	6.
2 S. Staffs	3.
9 H.L.I.	2.
1 Herts	1
1 K.R.R.	1
2 Gren Gds	1
R.E. 11 Fd. Co	3
1 R. Berks	3
1 H.L.I.	1
1 Kings	1
2 Ins Fus.	3.
7 Kings	1
	34

Prevailing Disease —
Admitted with Dropsy —

Evacuated M.A.C.
Officers. 61
Other Rks. – 241
Ret'd Duty
Officers —
Other Rks. —
Light Duty
Other Rks. 34

		Sick	Wnd.
Admitted	Officers	2	49.
"	Other Rks.	—	189
Evac'd	Officers	2	~~47~~ 59
"	Other Rks.	14	~~[illegible]~~ 241
Remng.	Officers	—	35
"	Other Rks.	13	117

P H Lloyd Jones

Capt. RAMC.
A.D.M.S. 2nd Divn. O.C. No. 4 Fd. Ambce.

List of officers admitted will follow.

Roll of officers admitted No 4 Fd Ambce
24 hrs ended 9 a.m. 18/5/15

Lieut. J. I. F. Bournhillon, R.E. 11th Fd. Co. G.S.W. Back
" " H J Ticklees 2nd Oxfords " Arm
2nd Lt. R. Gambier-Parry, 1st R.W.F. Shell W. Hand.
Capt. L Leeson, R.G.A. 13th Sge. Batt. " " Head
Lieut. A. E. Messer 1st K.R.R., " " Hand
2nd Lt. F. M. C. Cames, 2nd Border " " Head
" " G. S. Barton, 1st R.W.F. " " Head
" " G. E. H Slater, 2nd Border G.S.W. Legs.
" " H. G. Byng, " " " Abdomen
" " R. E. V. Kyrinaston, 1st Kings Sprain Ankle.
" " C. S. Searle, 2nd Army att. 1 R. Berks G.S.W. Back.
Lieut. J Landuminal 2nd R. Scots att 8th. Shell W. Forearm
" H J Lyle 2nd. H.L.I. G.S.W. Head
Capt. K. W. Lee, R.F.A. 12th. Batt. Sh. Wnd Cheek.
Lieut. A. L. Roche, 2nd R. Scots. Bay^t. W. Leg.
2nd Lt. A. Hague, 3rd Warks att R.E. 170 Co. Sh. W. Mouth.
Capt. R. H. Morgan, 2nd S. Staffs G.S.W. Scalp.
" H. E. Derington, " " " Arm.
Lieut. A. H. Ferguson, 7th London, Sh. W. Ankle.
" W. Kerr, 2nd Border G.S.W. Hip
" T. E. Alexander 2nd Wilts Sh. W. Chest & Back
" R. E. Hodgson, N. Staffs att 2. S. Staffs G.S.W. Ankle.
2nd Lt. R. Weir 8th. R. Scots " Leg.
Major G. T. A. Drought R.F.A. 51st. Batt. Sh. W. Shoulder.
Capt. J. G. Holtzapffell 7th London. G.S.W. Shock.
~~Lt.~~ 2nd Lt. R. A. Toller, 1st S. Staffs. Wound Concussion

2nd Lt. G. R. Brookless, 4 Camerons, Sh wnd Thighs
" " C. Dean 2nd Oxfords " " R. Knee
" " T. H. Lodge, 24th London " " Head
Lieut. J. B. Fowler, " " " " Chest.
Capt. A. L. M. Molesworth 8th Gurkhas " " Thigh
" R. McDonald 4th Camerons G.S.W. Neck.
2nd Lt. A. H. Penn, 2nd Gren. Gds. " Legs.
" " F. V. Parker, 2nd Bedfords. G.S.W. Side, Bay[t] Buttocks
" " R. H. Boys " " Sh. Wound Shdr. & Legs.
Lieut. C. Williams 2nd H. L. I. G.S.W. R. Knee.
2nd Lt. T. Chalmers, 4th Camerons Sh. wnd Shoulders.
Capt. A. B. Mackenzie, " " " " L. Thigh.
" E. G. Mylne, 1st. Irish Gds. G.S.W. L. Shdr. & Abdom.
2nd Lt. J. M. Benoy, 1st S. Staffs. " Scrotum & L. Thigh
" " C. R. Carruthers 4 Camerons " L. Leg.
Lieut. W. T. Quinlan, RAMC. (att 2. R. Scots) " L. Chest.
" M. Kincaid-Smith, 2nd H. L. I. " Back.
" A. J. Daish, 1st. Herts, " Face & Head
" F. W. Hardhaugh, 6th London, " R. Arm & Hip
" D. G. ~~[illegible]~~ Watson, RAMC. (att 2nd Bedfds) Shell wnds. R. Arm Shoulder & Leg.
Major H. B. Bottomley, 2nd Queens, Shell wnd Scalp & Chest
2nd Lt. L. S. C. Pease, 1st. Irish Guards, " " R. Hand
Lieut. E. W. Ward, 13th R. Highland Canadians
" R. M. Molesworth, 2nd Gordons, G.S.W. Thorax.
2nd Lt. G. R. M. Usney, 2nd Gordons, " Abdomen

P. K. Lloyd Jones
Capt. RAMC.
OC. No. 4 Fd Amb.

19/5/15.

Instructions regarding War Diaries and Intelligence Summaries are contained in F. S. Regs., Part II. and the Staff Manual respectively. Title pages will be prepared in manuscript.

WAR DIARY
or
~~INTELLIGENCE~~ SUMMARY.

(Erase heading not required.)

Army Form C. 2118.

Hour, Date, Place	Summary of Events and Information	Remarks and references to Appendices
19th May, 1915. BETHUNE.	The G. O. C. 1st. Corps visited the Dressing Station. H. R. H. The Prince of Wales visited the Officers' Dressing Station. Number of Casualties admitted - Officers 11 Other Ranks 116. Evacuated by No 7 M A C. Officers 17. Other Ranks 122.	PHG

No 4 Field Ambulance

Sick and wounded admitted, by Units, during 24 hours ended 9 a.m. 19/4/15.

Unit 2nd Divn	Officers Sick	Officers Wndd	Other Rks Sick	Other Rks Wndd
1st. Irish Guards.		10	3	86
2nd Grenadiers "		~~2~~ 3		16
R.F.A. 16 Batt.		1		
1st. Herts.		2		5
1st. Kings		4		10
4th "		1		15
5th "				4
7th "				1
2nd S. Staffs		1		2
2nd H.L.I.				4
1st. K.R.R.				1
2nd Innis Fus.				1
2nd Oxfords				2
2nd Worces.		1		1
3 Drag. Gds. att 1 Irish Gds.		1		
Total		23	3	148
Other Divs.				
4 Camerons.		2	1	2
RAMC. att 8 R. Scots.		1		~~4~~
R.F.A. 1st T.M. Batt.		1		
R. Montreal R.A.				1
1st. S. Staffs.		1		3
2nd Warwicks				2
16 Canadian Scott.		1		5
2nd Bedfords.	1	3		
14 Canadians		1		3
2nd Scots Gds.		1		9
2nd Yorks.				3
2nd Wilts.			2	1
Canad. Engrs 3 Fd Co.				1
R.E. 1st. Highland F. Co.				1
1st. R.M.F.		1		
2nd Gordons.				1
2nd Bl. Watch				4
1 H.L.I.		1		4
23 London	1			
7 "		1		
20 "		1		
2nd R. Scots.		1		
RAMC. 2 Fd. Amb.	1			
15th London		1		
R.F.A. 12. Batt.		1		
~~"~~ 8 R. Scots		3		4
Germans.		1		8
Total.	3	22	3	52

Light Duty

9 H.L.I.	3
2 "	11
2 S. Staffs	9
1 R. Berks	2
1 K.R.R.	5
1 Kings	3
R.F.A. 44 Bty.	1
2 Worces	1
2 Oxfds	1
R.G.A.	1
	37

Prevailing Disease - Nil
Admitted with Dropsy - Nil

		Sick	Wndd
Admitted	officers	3	45
"	Other Rks.	6	200
Evac'd	officers	3	50
	Other Rks.	7	203
Remaining	officers	–	30
"	Other Rks.	6	114

Evac'd M.A.C.

officers 53
Other Rks. 173

Returned Duty

officers –
Other Rks. –

Light Duty

Other Rks. 37.

P. H. Lloyd Jones
Capt. RAMC
OC. No. 4 Fd. Ambce.

ADMS. 2nd Dn.
19/5/15.

No. 14 [illegible] Ambulance.

[illegible] of officers admitted 24 hours [illegible] 9 a.m.

19/5/15.

2nd Lieut. R. S. [illegible] [illegible],	1st Irish Guards,	G.S.W. Head
" " C. R. Hughes,	2nd R. Scots Fus.	[illegible]
" " M. Hall,	2nd S. Staffs.	" " L. Leg.
Lieut. G. M. Henderson,	1st H. L. I.	G.S.W. Arm.
" F. C. F. B[illegible]scoe,	2nd Worcs.	Shell wnd Abdomen & Arm.
2nd Lt. J. C. Thompson	4 Camerons	G.S.W. Testicles
Lieut. A. Groves	2nd Bedfords	" Abdomen
" C. F. Woodward	1st R. W. F.	Shell W. Back.
Capt. H. Beaumont,	2nd Scots Gds.	" " "
2nd Lt. S. G. Fallowes,	1st Irish Gds.	" " "
Capt. J. H. Baillie	4th Camerons	G.S.W. R. Thigh
Lieut. H. S. Kuhn	2nd Bedfords.	Shell W. R. Jaw
" W. E. McL. Steward,	2nd Bl. Watch	" " Buttock.
2nd Lt. A. F. Paterson,	4th Camerons	G.S.W. Arm.
" " G. Lindsey,	5th R. Scots.	Shell W. Arm
Lt. Col. A. Brook,	—do—	G.S.W. Head
" " Lord Henry Scott,	23rd London,	[illegible]
Lieut. Tims, R. D. M.,	7th London	Wound [illegible]
2nd Lt. A. L. Thomas,	20th London,	" "
Capt. G. M. Smith	[illegible] att 8 R Scots.	Shell wnd Head
" E. Saunders,	R. F. A. 1st T. M. Batt.	" " Arm Thigh
" F. H. Palmer,	1st Herts.	" " Chin

" [illegible] de Persse	" " "	" " Face
Major The Earl of Rosse	" " "	" " Head
2nd Lt. J. R. M. Green	3rd Dragoons att Irish	" " Leg & Arm

Lieut J. M. Reid,	16th Canadian Scottish.	Shell wnd Arm.
" H. B. Timmins	1st. S Staffs	" " Head & Leg
2nd Lt. R. Paget	1st. Irish Guards	G. S. W. Arm.
Capt. G. E. S. Young	" "	" R. Hand
Major R. R. Reid	" "	Wnd Concussion
2nd Lt. Lardner R. S.,	2nd Bedfords	G. S. W. R. Thigh.
2nd Lt. E. M. Campbell	1st. Irish Guards	Shell wnd Jaw
Lieut A. B. Dervicke-Jones,	1st. Kings,	G. S. W. Head
Lieut J. F. Christie	1st. Herts	Shell wnd Head
2nd Lt. A. A. Jamason,	8th. R. Scots	" " R. Arm
" " Hon. Philip Cary,	2nd Gren. Gds.	G. S. W. R. Arm & Buttock
" " J. R. Ralli	1st. Irish Gds.	G. S. W. L. Hip
" " C. F. V. Fulton	1st. Kings	" R. Foot R. Shoulder
Capt. S. E. Norris	" "	Shell wnd Head
Lieut H. M. Hutchinson	" "	" " R. Arm & Head
Capt. G. H. Jenkins	4th. Kings	G. S. W. Chest (Slight)
Lieut Col. W. R. A. Smith,	2nd Gren. Gds.	G. S. W. Head.
2nd Lieut C. C. Creed,	2nd Gren. Gds.	" R. Elbow
~~Lieut~~ Lieut C. B. Price	14th. Canadians	Sh. wnd Buttock & Hand
2nd Lt. B. H. Hardy,	2nd Bedfords	N. Y. D.
" " R. A. S. Hodgins	R. F. H. 12th Batt	Concussion
" " F. Cavanagh	" 16th " ×	"
Lieut The Hon H. S. Alexander	1st. Irish Gds ×	G. S. W. Neck.

D. H. Lloyd Jones

ADMS 2nd Div · Capt. RAMC

19/5/15. · OC No 4 Fd Ambce

Instructions regarding War Diaries and Intelligence Summaries are contained in F. S. Regs., Part II. and the Staff Manual respectively. Title pages will be prepared in manuscript.

WAR DIARY

or

~~INTELLIGENCE SUMMARY.~~

(*Erase heading not required.*)

Army Form C. 2118.

Hour, Date, Place	Summary of Events and Information	Remarks and references to Appendices
20th May, 1915. BETHUNE.	Capt. G. E. Dyas, RAMC and B Section Bearer Sub-Divn returned to Headquarters.	
	The 12 cases that had been under treatment by Capt. Addinsell and the 12 observation cases were evacuated to No 4 Casualty Clearing Station today. The experiments were very satisfactory. Cresol Paste appears to be of great value, though it would be better to try it under more adverse circumstances, and to wait for a longer period until considerably more cases had been done.	PHG
	No. of casualties - Officers 16. Other Rks 57.	
	Evacuated by No 7 M.A.C. Officers 10 Other Rks. 47.	

(73989) W4141—463. 400,000. 9/14. H.&J.Ltd. Forms/C. 2118/10.

No. 4 Field Ambulance.

No. of sick and wounded admitted during 24 hours ended 9 a.m. 20/5/15

Unit - 2nd Division.	Officers Sick	Officers Wndd	Other Rks. Sick	Other Rks. Wndd
2nd Grenadier Guards.				11
1st. Irish Guards.		2		18
3rd Coldstream Guards.			1	1
1st. Herts.		1	-	30
1st. Kings.				1
7th. "				9
4th. "				1
Total.	—	3	1	71
Other Divisions				
1st. H. L. I.				4
1st. Queens.				2
14th Canadians				8
1st. S. Staffs.				2
23rd London	1			
2nd Bedfords.				1
15 Sepoys.				1
2nd Wilts.		1		
7th. London		1		
14th. R. Montreal				1
4th Canadian Hdrs.				2
15th Canadians				4
16th Canadians				3
13th Canadians.			1	1
2nd R. Scots.			1	
17th. Canadians.				1
R.F.A. 7th. DAC.			1	
2nd Yorks.				3
5th. R. Hdrs.				1
R.FA. 106 Batty.				1
A.S.C. att 1/4 Gurkhas.			1	
20th. London.	1			
19th. London.		2		
Germans.				5
15th Sikhs		1		
1/5 Seaforths		1		
Total.	2	6	4	40

To Lt. Duty

1 Kings	2
7 "	5
4 "	2
16 Canadns	1
2 Gren Gds.	1
1 Irish "	12
1 Herts	3
14 Canads.	2
1 H.L.I.	1
2 Bl. Wch.	1
2 Yks.	1
2 Wilts	2
	33

To Duty

2 H.L.I.	1.
2 Oxfds.	1.
4 Camerons	1
	3

Evac'd by M.A.C.
Officers 17
Other Rks. 122

Returned Duty
Officers —
Other Rks. 3

~~Evac'd~~ **Retd Lt Duty**
Other Rks. 33

Evac'd to Barges
Officers } Nil.
Other Rks. }

Prevailing Disease - Admitted with dropsy.

	Sick	Wnd.
Admitted officers	2	9
" Other Rks.	5	111
Evacuated officers	1	16
" Other Rks.	2	121
Remaining officers	1	23
" Other Rks.	9	69

[illegible signature]

No 4 Field Ambce
Roll of Officers admitted 24 hrs ended
9 am 20/5/15

2nd Lt R.D. Oldham,	1st Herts	×	Wnd. Concussion
" " A P Halcrow	23rd London	✓	Influenza
Lieut Sir G A Burke,	1st Irish Guards	✓	G.S.W. Head
2nd Lt. H M Yeatman,	2nd Wilts.	✓	Shell wnd Back.
" " A.R.K. Aitkens,	7th London.	✓	" " {Hands & legs
" " A.W.L. Paget,	1st Irish Guards.	✓	" " Back
Capt. H.C. Honeybourne,	20th. London,	✓	Diarrhoea
J.J. Pass,	19th. London.	✓	Shell wnd {R. Leg & R. Foot
" F.C. Waterfield	15th. Sikhs	✓	" " Head
Lieut J Mutter	1/5 Seaforths	✓	G.S.W. Face & Hand
2nd Lt. C.H. Westendarp	19th London	✓	Wnd Concussion

P. A. Lloyd Jones

Capt RAMC
OC. No 4 Field Ambce.

20/5/15.

Instructions regarding War Diaries and Intelligence Summaries are contained in F. S. Regs., Part II. and the Staff Manual respectively. Title pages will be prepared in manuscript.

WAR DIARY
or
~~INTELLIGENCE SUMMARY.~~
(Erase heading not required.)

Army Form C. 2118.

Hour, Date, Place	Summary of Events and Information	Remarks and references to Appendices
21st May, 1915 BETHUNE	Capt. H. Mc H. McCullagh and C Section Bearer Sub-Division returned to Headquarters. During the evening several shells were dropped into BETHUNE, in the vicinity of the Hospital, one bursting at the entrance gate, severely wounding No. 920 Pte Wells RAMC on ~~duty~~ police duty. No 9037 Pte Wood, RAMC, was also wounded in the leg whilst on duty in the town. All patients in Hospital were evacuated at 8.45 pm. Also all patients in the Officers' Dressing Station. Verbal orders to this effect were given by A.D.M.S. 2nd Dvn after the evacuation had taken place. Number of Casualties – Officers 7. Other Rks. 17. Evacuated by No 7 M.A.C. Officers 37. Other Ranks 81. Evacuated to Barges – 37 Other Ranks.	PHG.

(73989) W4141—463. 400,000. 9/14. H.&J.Ltd. Forms/C. 2118/10.

No. 4 Field Ambulance

Officers and other Rks admitted sick and wounded, by Units, during 24 hours ended 9a.m. 21/5/15.

Unit – 2nd Divn.	Officers Sick	Officers Wndd	Other Rks Sick	Other Rks Wndd
2nd Colds. Gds.		1	3	7
3rd "				6
1st Irish "				1
1st Herts.				1
~~1st Kings~~				
" " att 4th.	1			
4th "				2
5th "			1	
1st R. Berks.			1	
Total	1	1	5	17
Other Divs.				
2nd Gurkhas				1
1st H.L.I.				1
10th Canadians		1		
13th " Scott.		3		3
14th Canadians				9
16th " Scott.		1		1
15th Canadians			2	
6th London	1	1		
8th London	1			
15th London	1	[illegible]		
8th Argyle & Suth. Hdrs.		1		
1/5 Seaforths		1		
1/6 Seaforths.			1	2
8th Batt. 90th Canad. Rfls.				1
2nd Warwicks.	1			
R.F.A. 54th Bde.			1	
" 1st T.M. Batt.			1	
" 9th Batt.		1		
R.H.A. X Batt.			1	
West Rdg. Hows. B.A.C.			1	
R.G.A. 12th Bde.	1			
R.A.M.C. 47th Lond D. San Sec.				1
A.V.C. 7th Divn				1
48th Canadn Hdrs.				1
Germans.				1
Total.	5	9	7	22

To Duty

A.S.C. 1.
R.G.A. 1.
2

Light Duty

7 Kings 1.
3 R. Hdrs. 2.
1 Irish Gds. 2.
1 Meerut Divn 1.
6

Evac'd by M.A.C.

Officers 10
Other Rks. 47

Retd Duty

Officers –
Other Rks. 2

Retd Lt Duty

Other Ranks. 6

Prevailing Disease
Admitted with Dropsy

	Sick	Wndd
Admitted officers	6	10
" other Rks.	12	39
Evac'd officers	1	9
" other Rks.	–	47
Remng. officers	7	23
" other Rks.	20	57

Nominal Roll of officers admitted 24 hrs. ended 9 am. 21/5/15.

Capt. A. Leigh-Bennett, D.S.O.,	2nd Colds. Gds.	✓	Sh. wnd Head.
" H. G. Lee-Warner,	9th. Batt. R.F.A.	✓	G.S.W. R. Wrist.
2nd. Lt. A. F. W. Hewson,	1st. att. 4th Kings.	✓	Neurasthenia
Capt. A. Campbell,	8th. Argyle & S. Hdrs.	✓	Sh. wnd L. Hand
2nd Lt. L. Clark,	1/5th. Seaforths	✓	G.S.W. L. Arm
Lieut. S. B. Skevington	18th. London	✓	N.Y.D.
2nd Lt. W. D. Brockman,	8th. London	✓	Neurasthenia
" " E. J. W. Noakes,	6th. London	✓	Diarrhoea
Lieut C. M. Horsey	13th. Canadians	✓	Shell W. R. Arm.
Capt. C. T. Costigan,	10th. "	✓	G.S.W. Head
" E. M. Sellon,	13th. "	✓	" Groin
Lieut W. D. Smith,	13th. "	✓	Sh. W. R. Arm
~~Capt.~~ Lieut A. J. Gray	16th. "	✓	G.S.W. Arm
2nd Lt. A. E. French	6th. London	✓	Sh. W. R. Arm
Capt. J. Rothwell,	2nd Warwicks	✓	Neurasthenia
" A. J. Waring,	R.G.A. 12th. Bde	✓	Diarrhoea

P. H. Lloyd Jones

Capt. RAMC
O.C. No. 4 Fd. Ambce.

A.D.M.S. 2nd. Divn
21/5/15.

Army Form C. 2118.

Instructions regarding War Diaries and Intelligence Summaries are contained in F. S. Regs., Part II. and the Staff Manual respectively. Title pages will be prepared in manuscript.

WAR DIARY
or
INTELLIGENCE SUMMARY.

(Erase heading not required.)

Hour, Date, Place	Summary of Events and Information	Remarks and references to Appendices
22nd May, 1915 BETHUNE and LAPUGNOY	The following order was received from D.A.D.M.S. 2nd Divn. "O.C. No 4 F.A. O.C. No 5 F.A. O.C. No 6 F.A. M.D. 716. 22. The following moves will take place forthwith:- No 4 F.A. Hd. Qrs. and A. Section to LAPUGNOY (Parish Hall) B Section to LABEUVRIERE (School) C " " VENDIN-LEZ-BETHUNE (School). No. 5 F.A. The section now at LAPUGNOY will rejoin Head Qrs. of its Unit at ALLOUAGNE. No 6 F.A. Will march via CHOCQUES to the road junction in V27a and there await orders. The O.C. will notify by bearer the approximate time he will arrive at this point.	PHL
A.D.M.S. 2nd Divn. 8.15 am.	(Signed) O. Ievers Major. D.A.D.M.S. 2 Divn.	

(73989) W4141—463. 400,000. 9/14. H.&J.Ltd. Forms/C. 2118/10.

Instructions regarding War Diaries and Intelligence Summaries are contained in F. S. Regs., Part II. and the Staff Manual respectively. Title pages will be prepared in manuscript.

WAR DIARY

or

~~INTELLIGENCE SUMMARY~~.

(*Erase heading not required.*)

Army Form C. 2118.

Hour, Date, Place	Summary of Events and Information	Remarks and references to Appendices
22nd May, 1915 LAPUGNOY (Continued)	By 2 pm. all three sections had moved from the Hospital at BETHUNE to their various positions. A Section arrived at LAPUGNOY and opened a ~~Hospital~~ Dressing Station with accommodation for 60 sick at the Parish Hall. The men were bivouacked on a hill at the back of the Hospital. As the weather was perfect the ~~men~~ enjoyed this. C Section opened a ~~Hospital~~ Dressing Station PAG at VENDIN-LEZ-BETHUNE with accommodation for 50 patients. This accommodation could be increased to 80 if necessary. B Section opened a ~~Hospital~~ Dressing Station PAG in the Schools at LABEUVRIÈRE with accommodation for 50 patients which might be extended in an emergency. Cpl Steele RAMC and a party of 8 men remained behind at BETHUNE to guard the equipment which was left behind at the Civil and Military Hospital. Instructions were sent to him to mark both entrances to the Main Dressing Station, the entrance to the Officers Dressing Station, the RAMC Officers Billet, and the ~~[illegible]~~ gate of the field in which the wagons were parked with the words No. 4 Field Ambce. Cpl Steele reported that this had been done. Cpl Steele was, later, ordered to place men in each of these positions.	PAG.

(73989) W4141—463. 400,000. 9/14. H.&J.Ltd. Forms/C. 2118/10.

Army Form C. 2118.

Instructions regarding War Diaries and Intelligence Summaries are contained in F. S. Regs., Part II. and the Staff Manual respectively. Title pages will be prepared in manuscript.

WAR DIARY
or
~~INTELLIGENCE SUMMARY.~~
(Erase heading not required.)

Hour, Date, Place	Summary of Events and Information	Remarks and references to Appendices
22nd May, 1915. LAPUGNOY. (Continued)	The Brigade Major, 4th Guards Brigade was notified of my dispositions. The Headquarters of 4th. Gds. Brigade is ½ mile S.W. of the town. Headquarters of A.D.M.S. at LABEUVRIÈRE. The Commanding Officer issued the following special order. "The Commanding Officer wishes to express his appreciation of the orderly way in which all ranks carried out their duties during the evacuation of wounded from the Hospital at BETHUNE on the evening of the 21st. instant."	[signature]

No 4 Field Ambulance

Nos. of sick and wounded admitted during 24 hours ended 9am. 22/5/15.

Units 2nd Divn	Officers Sick	Officers Wnd	Other Rks. Sick	Other Rks. Wnd
2nd Coldm. Gds.			5	1
R.E. 170th Co.		1		
R.A.M.C. 4 F.A.				1
1st Herts	1			
Total	1	1	5	2
Other Divns				
22nd London		1		
13th Canadians			1	3
14th ″		1	1	1
5th ″		1		
7th London	1			
20th ″	1			1
21st ″	1			
4th Gordons	[illegible]		1	
6th ″			1	
Amb. 5th Lon F.A.				1
Total.	2	3	4	6

Evac'd M.A.C.

Officers 37

Other Rks. 81

Evac'd Barge

Officers Nil

Other Rks 13.

Duty

Nil.

To Duty

Nil.

	Sick	Wnd
Admitted Offrs.	3	4
Other Rks.	9	8
Evac'd Officers	10	27
Other Rks.	29	65
Remaining Off.	—	—
Other Rks	—	—

2nd Lt.	A.F. BUTALAY,	22nd London	G.S.W. Foot.
″ ″	H.D. MARTIN,	R.E. 170th Coy.	″ L. Shldr.
Lieut.	D.E. WARD,	7th London	N.Y.D.
2nd Lt.	R.R. LLOYD,	1st Herts	N.Y.D.
Lieut.	H. WE ARNE,	8th Canadians	Shell Shock
2nd Lt.	R.M. ROBERTS,	5th Gordons	Bruised hand
Lieut.	W.M. PEARCE,	14th Canadians	Sh. wound back

[illegible signature]

Capt. R.A.M.C.

O.C. No. 4 F.Amb.

A.D.M.S. 2nd Divn

Instructions regarding War Diaries and Intelligence Summaries are contained in F. S. Regs., Part II. and the Staff Manual respectively. Title pages will be prepared in manuscript.

WAR DIARY

or

~~INTELLIGENCE SUMMARY.~~

(*Erase heading not required.*)

Army Form C. 2118.

Hour, Date, Place	Summary of Events and Information	Remarks and references to Appendices
23rd May, 1915. LAPUGNOY.	A car ~~was~~ is sent daily by No 7 M. A. C. for any evacuations. Should more than one car be required a note is sent, by the driver of the car, to OC No. 7 M.A.C., intimating the number of cars required.	
	Number of casualties - 4 sick.	
	2nd Lieut Viscount Cranbourne, 2nd Grenadier Guards was sent to Lillers (No 4 Casualty Clearing Station) for examination & treatment of his ears.	
	The Commanding officer inspected C Section.	
24th May, 1915. LAPUGNOY.	The DDMS 1st Corps inspected the Dressing Station today.	
	Weather continues perfect and the men are all enjoying, and feeling the benefit of the rest, after their hard work at BETHUNE.	
	Number of casualties admitted, 9 sick all of whom were evacuated by No. 7 M A C.	
	The following men proceeded for duty with the units stated against their names:- No. 9024 Pte Walton S. RAMC 1st R Berks Regt. " 47830 " Lumley T. " 41st Bde. R F A. " 34845 " Neasham B " 2nd Gren. Gds.	
	~~Pte~~ No. 6373, Pte Busby A., RAMC arrived for duty from 2nd Grenadier Guards.	[initials]

No 4 Field Ambulance

No of sick & wounded by Units admitted during 24 hours ended 9 am 23/5/15.

Units 2nd Div	Officers		Other Ranks		Remarks
	Sick	Wounded	Sick	Wounded	
1st Irish Gds	.	.	2	4	
1st Kings	.	.	1	.	
2nd South Staffs	.	.	.	1	
Total	.	.	3	5	.
Other Divisions	Nil		Nil	Nil	
Total	.	.	.	.	

Evacd by 7 M.A.C. – Nil
Retd to Light Duty – Nil
" " Duty – Nil

	S	W
Admitted Officers	.	.
" Other Rks	3	5
Remaining Officers	.	.
" Other Rks	3	5

P R Lloyd Jones

A.D.M.S
2 Div. 9 am
23/5/15

Capt R.A.M.C.
O.C. No 4 Fd Amb

No. 4 Field Ambulance.

Officers & Other Ranks admitted wounded during 24 hrs ended 9 p.m. 23rd

British		German		Remarks
Officers	Other Rks	Officers	Other Rks	
Nil	Nil	Nil	Nil	

P. A. Lloyd Jones.
Capt. R. Amb.
O.C. No. 4 Fd Amb.

A.D.M.S.
2 Div 9 pm
23/5/15

Instructions regarding War Diaries and Intelligence Summaries are contained in F. S. Regs., Part II. and the Staff Manual respectively. Title pages will be prepared in manuscript.

WAR DIARY
or
~~INTELLIGENCE SUMMARY.~~
(*Erase heading not required.*)

Army Form C. 2118.

Hour, Date, Place	Summary of Events and Information	Remarks and references to Appendices
25th. May, 1915. LAPUGNOY.	The Commanding Officer inspected B. Section at LABEUVRIÈRE today. The 4th. Guards Brigade moved off at 6 o'clock this evening. Weather continues perfect. No. 5766 Cpl. Stacey, G. A., RAMC arrived for duty from 1st. R. Berks Regt. No casualties admitted today. No. 12691 Cpl. Ahearn W., RAMC arrived for duty from 41st. Bde. R.F.A. Rev. C. F. Baines, proceeded for duty with 14th Dvn. No. 12495 Pte Andrey A., 3rd Coldstream Guards proceeded with Rev. C. F. Baines, to 14th Dvn., as batman.	
26th. May, 1915. LAPUGNOY.	Weather still good. Casualties admitted - 2 sick both of whom were evacuated. No. 923 Pte Lewis J. proceeded to 1st. Kings Regt. for duty No 5050 Cpl Birtwistle W., RAMC proceeded for duty to 1st. R. Berks Regt. No 2571 Cpl. Webb J. RAMC proceeded to 41st. Bde. RFA. for duty.	PHG

No. 4 Field Ambce.

No. of Officers and other Ranks admitted, by Unit during 24 hours ended 9am. 25/5/15.

2nd Divn	Officers		Other Rks.	
	Sick	Wnd.	Sick	Wnd.
1st Irish Gds.			1	2
2nd Coldst. Gds.			1	
3rd "			1	
M.M.P.			1	
1st Herts.			3	
			7 *	2.

Evac by M.A.C.
Officers Nil
Other Rks 9.

Admitted Officers Nil
" Other Rks. 7. 2.
Evac Officers Nil
" Other Rks 7 2.
Remaining Officers Nil
" Other Rks Nil.

* All these sick were evacuated from 2nd RW Area.

P. A. Lloyd Jones
Capt. RAMC.
OC. No 4 Fd. Ambce

ADMS. 2nd Div.

No 4 Field Ambulance.

Sick and wounded admitted during 24 hours ended 9am. 26/5/15.

Unit.	Officers		Other Ranks.		
	Sick	Wndd	Sick	Wndd	
Nil					

P. H. Lloyd Jones

Capt. RAMC
OC. No 4 Field Ambce

ADMS 2nd Divn
26/5/15.

Instructions regarding War Diaries and Intelligence Summaries are contained in F. S. Regs., Part II. and the Staff Manual respectively. Title pages will be prepared in manuscript.

WAR DIARY

or

~~INTELLIGENCE SUMMARY.~~

(*Erase heading not required.*)

Army Form C. 2118.

Hour, Date, Place	Summary of Events and Information	Remarks and references to Appendices
27th May, 1915. LAPUGNOY.	Number of ~~casualties~~ admissions PHJ - 20 Sick, all of whom were evacuated. Weather still good but has turned much colder.	
28th May, 1915. LAPUGNOY.	Commanding Officer inspected B and C Sections today. The French Red Cross Society have taken over the building in which the officers' Dressing Station was situated in BETHUNE. Number of ~~casualties~~ admissions PHJ - 18 sick, all of whom were evacuated.	
29th. May, 1915. LAPUGNOY	Number of ~~casualties~~ admissions PHJ - 33 sick all of whom were evacuated. Weather continues cold but fine.	PHJ
30th May, 1915. LAPUGNOY.	Number of ~~casualties~~ admissions PHJ 33 sick, all of whom were evacuated	

No 4. Field Ambulance.

Sick and wounded admitted during 24 hours. ended 9 am 28/5/15

Unit 2nd Div.	Officers		Other Ranks		
	Sick	Wounded	Sick	Wounded	
Divl Mounted Troops			1		
1/ Herts Rgt.			4		Light Duty
2/ H. L. I.			2		Gren Gds. 1.
R.A.M.C. No 4 Fd A.			1		1 Irish Gds 1
3 Colds Gds.			2		
1 Irish Gds.			4		
2 Gren Gds.			3		
	-	-	20	-	

Evac by M.A.C.
Officers NIL
Other Ranks. 18
Light Duty 2.

admitted officers -
other Ranks 20
Evac officers -
other Ranks 18
Remaining officers -
other Ranks -

A.D.M.S.
2nd Div

P. H. Lloyd Jones
Capt. R.A.M.C.
OC. No 4 Field Ambl.

No 4. Field Ambulance.

Sick and wounded admitted during 24 hours ended 9 am 28/5/15.

Unit 2nd Div	Officers		Other Ranks		
	Sick	Wounded	Sick	Wounded	
2 Grenadier Gds.			4		
1 Irish Gds			1		
2 Coldstream Gds			1		
3 Coldstream Gds			1		
1 Herts.			2		
1 Kings Liv.			1		
4 Kings "			1		
2 South Staffs			3		
2 Worcesters			2		
South Irish Horse			1		
RFA 56 Batty			1		
	–	–	18*	–	

Evac by M A C
Officers NIL
other R. 18.

* All these sick were evacuated from 2nd Div area.

admitted Officers NIL
" other R. 18
Evac officers –
other R. 18
Remaining officers –
other R. –

ADMS.
29-5-15

P A Lloyd Jones
Capt R.A.M.C.
OC No 4 Field Amb

No 4 Field Ambulance.

Sick & wounded admitted during 24 hours ending 9 am 30-5-15.

Unit 2nd Div.	Officers Sick	Officers Wounded	Other Ranks Sick	Other Ranks Wounded	
2/Grenadier Gds.			3		
2 Coldstream Gds			2		
3 — "			1		
1 Irish Guards			4		
1 Herts.			4		
2 S Staffs			4		
RFA 15 Batty			1		
2/Worcesters			3		
2 Inniskilling F			1		
R.E. 5 F Coy			1		
5/Kings			1		
1/Kings			1		
1 KRR			1		
1 Berks.			1		
2 Ox & Bucks			2		
	–	–	* 33	–	

Evac by M.A.C.
officers NIL
other R 33

* all these sick evacuated from 2 Div area.

[illegible] -5.15

admitted officers –
other R. 33
Evac officers –
other R 33
Remaining officers
other R –

P A [illegible]
Capt RAMC
O.C. No 4 Fd Amb

Instructions regarding War Diaries and Intelligence Summaries are contained in F. S. Regs., Part II. and the Staff Manual respectively. Title pages will be prepared in manuscript.

WAR DIARY
or
~~INTELLIGENCE SUMMARY.~~

(*Erase heading not required.*)

Army Form C. 2118.

Hour, Date, Place	Summary of Events and Information	Remarks and references to Appendices
31st. May, 1915 LAPUGNOY	In accordance with Sec. Order W402 of 30th instant, issued by Commanding Officer C Section joined B Section at LABEUVRIERE. The following is a copy of the order:- "After departure of Guards Battalions from VENDIN and OBLINGHEM you will take your section to join C Section at LABEUVRIERE. Your billets are being arranged for you by OC. B Section 4 FA" ADMS 2nd Div. visited the Dressing Station and consulted with C.O. re providing accommodation for sick and wounded if necessary. An Officers Dressing Station was opened about ½ mile N. of the Dressing Station with accommodation for 4 Officers. The following accommodation was found in LAPUGNOY. Girls' School 80 beds* Boys School 80 beds.* Salle de Patronage 60 beds Private School 70 beds* making a total of 290 beds which could be increased to 300. At MARLES the following accommodation was found:- Ecole Libre des Mines - 150 beds* Ecole de Garçons 160 beds.* Salle de patronage - 50 " Ancien Ecole 50 " Ecole de Filles - 90 "* Isolation Ward 25 " Salle de Fêtes 40 beds Making a total of 565 beds. * Permission to use these buildings to be obtained from Sous-Prefet at BETHUNE.	

www.ingramcontent.com/pod-product-compliance
Lightning Source LLC
Chambersburg PA
CBHW081433160426
43193CB00013B/2268
* 9 7 8 1 4 7 4 5 0 3 3 7 2 *